Discovering

Jazz Dance

America's Energy and Soul

Discovering
Jazz Dance
America's Energy and Soul

Janice LaPointe-Crump
Kimberly Staley

Championship Series

WCB Brown & Benchmark

Book Team

Editor *Chris Rogers*
Production Coordinator *Kay Driscoll*

A Division of Wm. C. Brown Communications, Inc.

Vice President and General Manager *Thomas E. Doran*
Executive Managing Editor *Ed Bartell*
Director of Marketing *Kathy Law Laube*
National Sales Manager *Eric Ziegler*
Marketing Manager *Pamela S. Cooper*
Advertising Manager *Jodi Rymer*
Managing Editor, Production *Colleen A. Yonda*
Manager of Visuals and Design *Faye M. Schilling*

Production Editorial Manager *Vickie Caughron*
Publishing Services Manager *Karen J. Slaght*
Permissions/Records Manager *Connie Allendorf*

Wm. C. Brown Communications, Inc.

Chairman Emeritus *Wm. C. Brown*
Chairman and Chief Executive Officer *Mark C. Falb*
President and Chief Operating Officer *G. Franklin Lewis*
Corporate Vice President, Operations *Beverly Kolz*
Corporate Vice President, President of WCB Manufacturing *Roger Meyer*

Cover photo by Halsey Creative Services, Inc.

Interior design by Shelia K. Sabers

Copyeditor *Rosemary Wallner*

Library of Congress Catalog Card Number: 91–70692

ISBN 0–697–11392–2

Printed in the United States of America by Wm. C. Brown Communications, Inc., 2460 Kerper Boulevard, Dubuque, IA 52001

10 9 8 7 6 5 4 3 2 1

Contents

5 Principles of Dance Technique: Applications for the Jazz Dancer 73

Preface

The art of dance began with a single idea that was communicated by a simple non-verbal, bodily gesture. Over the centuries, as societies developed intricate rituals, many dance forms emerged. Through dancing people may contemplate, celebrate, mourn, and offer thanks in a formalized way. Although each form of dance is unique to a time and culture, each one holds a universal message that bridges the gap between past and present. All dance forms are linked because they share in the human experience and reflect the hopes and concerns common to humankind. How each gene emerged as a way for people to express themselves makes the study of different dance forms an exciting exploration into art and culture.

Jazz dance is especially well suited to communicate a perspective of the American social situation because it is so deeply rooted in contemporary American life. It is a folk art, meaning that it embodies easily recognizable non-verbal reactions to events that make up or are occurring in our society. Learning this form of dance brings with it direct satisfaction and pleasure. Jazz movement is powerfully accented and naturally syncopated.

In writing this book, we have intended to illuminate jazz dance as an art form, and to promote an appreciation of it. In this way, we hope you will understand the legacy of jazz as an original, uniquely American dance form. We have described the evolution of jazz steps and styles by drawing upon historical observations of the influences nurturing jazz to its present state. We've provided information about creating jazz choreography to promote your own creativity and curiosity about jazz as an expressive art form. These studies provide a way of passing on knowledge about ourselves and our culture.

This book is your guide to the exciting world of jazz dance. It is intended to encourage self-discovery and spontaneous interaction between you and your studio work. Each lesson will bring new challenges to meet and more accomplishments to realize. Throughout your dancing, stay in touch with your feelings and emotions. Make your jazz dancing a personal statement that is revealed within the movement. As you strive to improve your technique, keep in mind that the heart of jazz is the communication of the energy of a dancer's soul.

Music is a powerful element in jazz dance. It stimulates our senses and imagination by activating natural, rhythmic impulses. It is easy to get caught up in a tune with a steady even beat, especially if it is currently popular. Try not to fall into the "top ten" trap. Songs having a straight beat are often flat and repetitive. They often lack a true jazz feeling which is part of the expressive nature of this art form. Listen and dance to a variety of music that is innovative within the context of the jazz idiom. Jazz music embraces unusual rhythms reflecting a personal statement by the musicians. Music having little depth or personality will not encourage you to speak through your dancing. Don't neglect discovering both movement and music from the past. Styles of movement are sparked spontaneously in a given time and you will enjoy the experience of rediscovering the past through movement and music.

Dancing is a way to find ourselves through movement in a process of connecting the interior landscape of our mind with the external shapes of motion. In this way your self-knowledge will also lead to your understanding an important part of our American cultural heritage.

We wish to express our appreciation to the following for the use of photographs: The New York Public Library Performing Arts Research Center—Rita Waldron; Museum of Modern Art Still Archives—Terri Geesken; Jack Mitchell; Turner Entertainment; Bruce Davis' photography; Texas Woman's University and The Colony High School; and to all the companies that generously shared the images of their dancers and dances to enrich this book: American Dance Machine, Pepsi Bethel's American Authentic Jazz Dance Theatre, Arizona State University Department of Dance, Les Ballets Jazz de Montreal, Chi-town Jazz Dance, Al Germani Dance Company, Gus Giordano Jazz Dance Chicago, Joel Hall's Chicago Jazz Dance Theatre, Hubbard St. Dance Company, Jazzdance: The Danny Buraczeski Dance Company, Jazz Dance Theatre South, Jazz Tap Ensemble, San Francisco Jazz Dance Company, Southwest Jazz Ballet, Delia Stewart Dance Company, and Texas Woman's University Dance Repertory Theatre. To the dancers of Texas Woman's University—Christina Garcia, Margaret Fleming, Cha Cha Guerrero, Kimberly Harrison, Gina McGilvra, Erin Venable-Green, Linda Plumlee, Diana Rodriguez, Marta Salazar, and Lynelle Wessling; and to the dancers of The Colony High School—Jennifer Billings and Tracie Ward we are grateful.

To Tim and Gail who supported us more than they'll ever know. To Aileene S. Lockhart for her encouragement and editorial suggestions.

To Craig L. Turski, Kris Anthony, Gail Crump, and Wm. C. Brown Publishers, special thanks are extended for the original drawings they created for this book.

And to our students upon whose bodies and minds we burnished these ideas.

Janice LaPointe-Crump and Kimberly T. Staley
May, 1990

1

Introduction:
Jazz, the American Soul

Welcome to the world of jazz dancing. Like its musical counterpart, jazz is a uniquely American form of artistic expression. Jazz dancers blend styles and techniques of a number of other dance forms with contemporary music. These dancers are technically disciplined yet have a free, styled manner. Whether it's cool or hot, mellow or heavy, Broadway or Los Angeles in style, one thing is always clear: Jazz dance is an American original.

This book is a comprehensive guide for students who are new to jazz dancing or have not had much dance training. But what is jazz? How is it different yet similar to other kinds of dance? Let's begin here.

Defining Jazz Dance

In the *American Heritage Dictionary,* "Jazz" is defined as a musical term. Jazz music is characterized by strong, yet flexible rhythms. At its best, it employs highly sophisticated harmonics that result from spontaneously playing basic tunes and chord patterns. The listener can hear the exaggerated use of texture, harmony, and melody in these patterns. Jazz music attracts attention because of its immediate energy and direct strength.[1] A "radical" piece of music or performance is right on the beat, fresh, and almost wild.

Being fresh and almost wild is also an apt definition for jazz dancing. Having evolved gradually as an independent art form, it's difficult to define jazz dancing exactly. In 1917 the term "jazz" was coined to refer to African-American theatrical dancers who adapted their ethnic body isolations and rhythmic step patterns to European and Caribbean movements.[2] But if we limit jazz dance to a single definition, a rich heritage of creative

CHI-TOWN Jazz Dance Co.
Photo: Ron Pomerantz.

ingenuity and complex expression is ignored. Instead, let's think of jazz as a kind of theater dancing that is directly involved with popular, American culture. It is personified by an immediate, everyday yet formalized expression of contemporary life. Its various styles are founded upon particular rhythmic and dance step patterns. Because of this, some writers term jazz as "vernacular dancing." It's "groovy" in the same tradition as the music of Duke Ellington and Winston Marsalis; rhythms dominate lyrical phrases. What you see are the extremes rather than the subtleties of expression.

Jazz dance began to develop shortly after jazz music. Although it has flowered along with jazz music, since the 1920s, differing circumstances have affected jazz dancing. Dance is an ephemeral art form that depends upon an audience's response. Until the advent of film and video, it wasn't possible to save performances for someone to view at a later date. Consequently, dance images had to be instantaneously recognizable. While jazz music had the recording industry and radio to boost its popularity, jazz dance did not have that luxury. Jazz dance, therefore, emerged more slowly and has tended to be more directly linked to cultural fads. Consequently, jazz dance is almost chameleon in its constantly changing style. Laments writer Selma Jean Cohen, dance as a theatrical form seems almost unwilling "to stand still long enough to be examined."[3]

Today, jazz dance is universally popular and a powerful indicator of general taste. Jazz dance expression is not as deeply individualized as modern dance since jazz appeals and communicates to us in a universal way. It relates strongly to our sensory experiences and to our deepest emotional responses to life. Dancers use choreographic themes drawn directly from shared, cultural experiences and derived from emotional outpourings to which everyone can relate. There is a kind of tangible pleasure that is recognized early and expands with time.

Whether it's full of razzmatazz, street funk, cool, or heavy syncopation, jazz dancing is experienced by recognizing rhythms mentally and motion sensually. The use of counter tensions and astounding technique is mind-boggling. Exciting and exacting displays of raw technique and sudden changes in direction, foot work, and energy are most often linked to the unique style of the dancer, like a Paula Abdul or a Fred Astaire.

Quick to claim and absorb unusual and remarkable movement styles, jazz dance encourages experimentation. The source for the new and revolutionary has continued to be the spontaniety of the street dancer. Remember the Rockers group in the 1970s and break dancers in the 1980s? The strong acrobatic and intensely rhythmical movements were highly specialized and astounding. Gradually, the need for universality brought the sensational to more attainable standards of technique, style, and choreography. The residue of these exciting fads are movement motifs (jazz musicians call these *riffs*) that can contribute "awesome" creative movement ideas. Simplified fad elements have become part of the jazz dancer's vocabulary, contributing to its ever-changing complexion. The wildly innovative street dancer has always played this kind of role in the evolution of jazz style and form.

A dance student learns to join personalized "jiving" with formal ways of moving and expressing. There is much more to being a dancer than showing off. The late George Balanchine, a Broadway choreographer and founding artistic director of the New York City Ballet, said, "The dancer must show his mastery of muscular coordination. . . . [but] his presentation is an aesthetic manifestation [which] . . . should never be a piece of showmanship only to prove the dancer's muscular strength and technical skill."[4] Expressiveness and fluency enable the jazz dancer to go beyond mere showmanship.

How did jazz become this lively art and entertainment form? As Dolores Cayou, a noted African-American jazz teacher, asserts, the roots of jazz are embedded firmly in a bedrock of ethnic tradition. This tradition "is related to the total expression of a group of people and to their experience."[5]

The Roots of Jazz

Originally sacred and practical, dance in African tribal cultures existed as a fundamental way to communicate and celebrate. Not performing casually, dancers in Africa moved holistically. That is, the dancers felt deeply the religious or tribal functions of the dance as they were portrayed in their communal expressive act. Every movement, carried by various parts of the body simultaneously, consisted of complex rhythmic patterns that symbolized the dancer's relationship to nature.

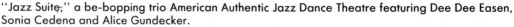

"Jazz Suite," a be-bopping trio American Authentic Jazz Dance Theatre featuring Dee Dee Easen, Sonia Cedena and Alice Gundecker.

Long held traditions are revealed in these dances. Even the musical instruments were constructed according to particular rules. Sacred bonds joined dancers and musicians as they demonstrated rhythmic interdependency. Underlying drum patterns were usually mirrored by the feet, then by the torso and through the limbs. The tribespeople moved with an active free pelvis and torso. Flat-footed, flex-kneed, and released hip postures rooted the dancers to the earth.

During the sixteenth century, Africans began arriving in America as slaves. They retained their style of moving, yet were influenced by the Euro-American culture in which they were forced to live.

The Euro-American culture was entrenched with the idea that the mind was superior to the body. Dancing, therefore, was relegated to a socializing role as entertainment and recreation. Dancing was not an attempt to communicate with the spiritual forces of life or to carry out a needed ritual. Instead the dancing could be rambunctious or politely genteel, depending upon the occasion. The gentry or their hired entertainers danced,

Jazz is the soul of American theater dance. San Francisco Jazz Dance Company
Photo: Casey Cartwright.

juggled, and sang all sorts of tunes, re-enacted stories, and told jokes. The forms had originated in stylized European and English peasant and court dances. These dances emphasized a quiet, erect spine and intricate, formal step patterns with little room for spontaniety. There was a tremendous contrast between these dances and the intentions, step patterns, and music of the slaves.

Slowly these individual rhythms, steps, and expressive elements were cross-fertilized, always reflecting the tempos of the times. Jazz dance, like jazz music, is now an indigenous American folk art that grew out of traditional African dance and ceremonials and Euro-American popular theater entertainment and social dance forms. The hot house for this hybridization took place in the early years of the twentieth century in cities like New Orleans, Chicago, New York, and Philadelphia. These and other cities experienced the greatest influx of African-Americans following Reconstruction.

Jack Cole, called the "father of jazz choreography," wrote in 1963 that jazz can never be ousted from its urban American home. It illuminates and comments upon the tensions and energy found in large cities. According to Cole, contemporary jazz is a theatricalized elaboration of the Lindy Hop, a social dance of the 1930s named for the famous aviator Charles Lindbergh.[6]

As its popularity grew, jazz amalgamated the training models and artistic principles of other dance forms: modern dance, tap, and classical ballet along with certain patterns borrowed from classical Indian dance and yoga. Never cautious, jazz dance will always be concerned with individual expression and formal variety.

Whether dressed up for the opera, borrowed from a Broadway musical, or blended for a TV special, jazz is perhaps the soul of American movement.[7] As the American spirit changes, so does its style and attitude. Consequently, formulating a single definition "can only destroy the balance, and reduce the jazz dance synthesis to a heap of individually meaningless movement remnants," writes jazz teacher Jean Sabatine.[8]

Intentions of This Book

If there is a single secret to achieving excellence as a jazz dancer, it is to think about and practice what is learned. Equally important is the will to seek additional knowledge about the art of jazz dancing. With that in mind, concepts and information, important to the dancer's experience, are the central driving forces behind this book. We asked ourselves these questions: What are the principles of movement that the dancer applies, first consciously and then intuitively, during the learning process? How are jazz dance and jazz music related? How are techniques and creative ideas from modern and ballet dancing applied in jazz? Who has made a lasting impact upon the development of jazz dancing?

This book brings to your fingertips the fundamental principles of dancing as interpreted for the jazz dancer. Your study of jazz dance will be enriched by the clear descriptions of the basic movements, steps, and patterns that form the foundation of jazz as a popular performance art. Throughout, we have emphasized the techniques and styles that are inherent in contemporary jazz. These techniques and styles are supported by traditional motifs and popular dance patterns from the past which remain a lively part of jazz technique. Included are those decisive classical ballet and modern dance movements that have been adapted and incorporated into jazz dance. Combined with the studio experience, this book describes and illustrates many of the primary concepts which identify dance as a rich, vigorous expressive language.

Since the imprint of each dancer's own style plays such an important role in jazz, we encourage you to personalize your dancing. Consequently, specific regional or school styles aren't stressed, rather you will find the classic elements. In this way, you will be informed and reminded of the fundamental techniques, traditional styles, primary choreographic methods, rhythmic patterns, aesthetic elements, and historical developments that have made jazz what it is today.

"Theme and Reflections" with music by Charles Mingus. Jazzdance: The Danny Buraczeski Dance Company.
Photo: Robin Holland.

As you seek information concerning the nature of jazz and the dance experience in general, you will find much more than an outline of jazz vocabulary. This book suggests a process which will carry you from practice to performance, from insight to expression.

This book concludes with a special feature, a videography of filmed musicals and other jazz-related programs. All are available at your local video rental store. No book is able to duplicate the unusual thrill of seeing a dancer subtly changing space, time, energy, or gesture. Seeing is believing. We urge you to supplement your reading and dancing by attending local performances and/or viewing recorded dance performances.

Common Sense First Aid Advice

Dancers learn to listen to and respect the body by understanding kinesiological and biomechanical principles of dance motion. How does the body move in relation to gravity and the laws of motion? Chapter Two presents an introduction to basic kinesiological and biomechanical concepts and includes a practical analysis of effective postural practices. A healthy and safe dance experience is an important goal. All the materials you find in this book have been designed to promote a positive mind-body experience.

Coping with muscle aches or minor soft-tissue injuries is one aspect of any human activity in which the body is challenged. When you perform movements repeatedly and work to increase flexibility or strength, common discomfort may persist for a few days. What should you do? First, some aches and tenderness are a normal by-product of moving dynamically, especially if you have been leading a fairly sedentary life or if you have been performing other forms of dance. Each motor experience develops the body and mind in specific ways. Consequently, a change in activity may result in a period of adjustment for the body. What follows represents accepted knowledge that anyone participating in vigorous physical exercise should know in order to move safely. (Do not rely upon this information to substitute for qualified medical attention and treatment.)

Be aware of early warning signs. If you experience pain that is hot and searing, if you seem to lose control of a body part, if you begin to sweat profusely and feel faint, if the discomfort continues for more than one week, see a qualified individual for treatment.

For localized pain at a joint or general pain in the center or belly of a muscle, there are immediate first aid procedures that you should follow.

RICE is an easy way to remember simple first aid for mild muscle and joint soreness or for similar injuries that occur in the studio.

Rest: Refrain from unnecessary physical activity until the discomfort ceases.

Ice: Apply an ice bag or a sealed baggie with ice to the injured area to reduce swelling. Keep the ice there for about 20 minutes until the affected area becomes bright red and numb. Do this twice a day until the discomfort subsides, usually about five days.

Compression: Wrap the area securely with an elastic bandage.

Elevation: Improve circulation and rest the body part on a horizontal level, propping the limb on a chair.

Sometimes an injury happens to the dancer who carefully warms up or who practices new movements carefully. What are the common injuries? Following are descriptions of the four most frequent types that beginning and intermediate level dance students may experience. These injuries usually involve the legs and feet.

Strain is a violent contraction of a muscle followed by a ripping sensation and a loss of stability in that area. You may not sense the injury until a few hours after it has occurred. Strains are usually accompanied by swelling, localized soreness, and muscle spasms. Rest and ice are the most common treatment. Avoid consecutive practicing of a new skill for long periods of time to help prevent this kind of injury.

Sprain is an injury to ligaments (the bands which hold and support joints) when they are suddenly and violently stretched. The outer part of the ankle and the inside part of the knee are most vulnerable. To avoid this kind of injury, do not invert or sickle the foot or bend the knees without aligning the knees over the ankles.

Shinsplints are considered the single most aggravating condition for a dancer. They can occur from dancing on overly hard surfaces, from jumping intensively, from dancing vigorously without first stretching the calves, and from landing without maintaining correct foot and leg alignment while softening the shock with the resistance of a plié.

A sharp, shooting pain is felt along the front of the calf. Sometimes there is an extremely tender point at the top of the arch of the foot, or a dull burning sensation on the outer part of the calf. Rest and ice are important partners in the treatment of shinsplints. Wearing one-half to one-inch heeled shoes reduces the work of the calf, allowing it to rest somewhat. Avoid leaps and jumps or rising to the balls of the feet during convalescence.

Achilles Tendinitis is an inflammation of the tendon characterized by extreme tenderness and swelling at the back of the ankle. Since a tendon is not elastic and does not contract, the Achilles tendon can be injured easily. Rest and ice for 20 minute periods twice daily is helpful as is wearing a one-half inch lift in your shoes. This is a stubborn kind of injury without a quick cure, other than full rest of the ankle and foot.

Dancing is an exciting and challenging enterprise. Certainly, injuries are not a common occurrence and should not be anticipated. Move with thoughtful care for your own body by performing steps accurately. Stretch tight muscles and strengthen the abdominals, feet, and calves. These measures remain the most effective ways to avoid being sidelined by an injury.

Welcome to the electric red, hot, and exuberant world of jazz dancing!

End Notes

1. *American Heritage Dictionary,* (2nd ed.), (Boston: Houghton Mifflin Company, 1982).
2. Horst Koegler, *The Concise Oxford Dictionary of Ballet,* (2nd ed.), (London: Oxford University Press, 1982).
3. Selma Jean Cohen, ''Review: Dance Index,'' *Journal of Aesthetics and Art Criticism,* Summer, 1972, *30,* p. 555.
4. Walter Sorrell, (Ed.), *The Dance Has Many Faces,* (New York: Columbia University Press, 1966), pp. 96–97.
5. Dolores Kirton Cayou, *Modern Jazz Dance,* (Palo Alto: National Press Books, 1971), p. xi.
6. Jack Cole, ''It's Gone Silly,'' in Gus Giordano's *Jazz Dance Anthology,* (Chicago: Orion Publishing House, 1975), p. 73.
7. William Como, Preface, in Gus Giordano's *Jazz Dance Anthology,* (Chicago: Orion Publishing House, 1975), p. iv.
8. Jean Sabatine, ''Jazz Dance: The American Hybrid,'' in Gus Giordano's *Jazz Dance Anthology,* (Chicago: Orion Publishing House, 1975), p. 110.

2

Taking A Dance Class:
The Studio Experience

Dressing for the Occasion

Dancing is a time for fun, experimentation, and exaggeration. Today, clothes that were once worn in the studio by dancers have now been adopted by the general public as ordinary street dress. When dressing for a jazz class, feel free to use bright dancewear. Personal taste and variety are the norm for the jazz class. Dancers wear parachute pants, shorts, and sweats, as well as the more traditional tights and leotard. Look at what the more experienced dancers in your school wear. If you have any doubts about the appropriateness of your class wear, consult your instructor.

No matter what you choose to wear, however, it is vitally important to have suitable supportive undergarments. Men must wear an athletic supporter under their tights or pants, and women should wear a bra. Remember that jazz is a physical experience. Broad sweeps of movement, athletic jumps, abrupt transfers of weight and direction, and quick changes in level finds the dancer in need of protective support to ensure safe dancing.

As for shoes, a number of manufacturers make jazz oxfords in leather or canvas in a variety of colors. Soles are either whole or split, and constructed of either pliable rubber or elk skin. Dance shoe look-alikes are popular, but they are intended for daily outdoor wear. They are not flexible enough for dancing. Some dancers wear lighweight sneakers. Going barefoot or wearing ballet shoes is not recommended, since neither gives the foot proper support or lift during off balanced movements, abrupt changes in level, or dynamic bursts of energy. Without good support, these forces are passed up through the leg to the knee and spine, inviting injury.

You are encouraged to shower following class, should such facilities be available. Besides cleansing the skin, water helps you cool off and encourages muscle relaxation following a vigorous work-out.

10

Ready for action.
TWU Dance Repertory Theatre.
Photo: Jennifer Collins.

Foot placement counts.
Photo: Jennifer Collins.

The First Lessons

The emptiness of a dance studio or gymnasium can appear imposing at first. Since we are more familiar with spaces that have been broken up by pieces of furniture, we can feel inhibited when faced with nothing but an expansive bare wood or vinyl floor.

Perhaps there are barres and full-length mirrors in your studio. Barres and mirrors are invaluable learning tools once you know how to use them effectively and objectively. A barre is used to balance yourself when you are learning new centers of gravity, to strengthen small muscle groups, and to support the stretching leg. The barre is used for reassurance. Never grip the barre. Rather, hold it easily. Rest your hand over the top of the barre holding the thumb in line with the wrist. Always stand in good alignment and avoid leaning on the barre, unless specifically instructed to do so.

Mirrors in a studio play an important function in the learning process. They enhance and accelerate the development of good postural habits and improve your view of the teacher. You're able to mirror the image that you observe. Try to forget whose reflection you are looking at. Look instead at your reflected image in an objective way.

When holding the barre correctly, the thumb is in line with the wrist.
Photo: Bruce Davis.

Holding the barre incorrectly.
Photo: Bruce Davis.

When beginning a dance class or learning a new step, be patient with yourself. Kinesthetic sensitivity and awareness of body placement develop gradually. Throughout each lesson, check for correct body positions, facing directions, and accurate step patterns. Frequent repetition of movements performed accurately and thoughtfully gives structure to your base of kinetic knowledge. Building a memory base of movement is one clear objective of a dance technique class that is enhanced when you begin to coordinate visual and auditory sensory cues. Thus you must relate your actual movements to the teacher's commands, to the explanations and descriptions, and to the musical accompaniment. The sensory impression you experience while performing the movement will improve. Motion combines with the expressive part of jazz dancing: *e-motion.*

The amount of pelvic release is determined by body structure, unless abdominals are weak or the dancer fails to engage them actively.
Photo: Bruce Davis.

Getting the Most from Your Class

As you enter the studio, release yourself from responsibility to others. You are accountable primarily to YOU. Put aside mental bundles: deadlines, relationships, and upcoming tasks. Seek ways to encourage your best efforts as you move. Avoid talking negatively to yourself. When you don't respect your own best efforts, you rob yourself of the opportunity to do even better. Remember this old but truthful adage: Success is achieved with 90% perspiration and only 10% inspiration and talent.

The "J" in jazz is for *joy*. This natural joy or "high" is made available to you when your time in class is used to experience life to its fullest. Come early to class in order to shed outer concerns before the lesson begins. Use this time to recall key concepts and review step patterns. This personal commitment is supported by moving through a personally designed ritual of body warm-ups to release undesirable muscular tensions. The result will be a freer use of the body and a faster rate of learning during the lesson. See Chapter Four for more information on warming up.

While a painter and musician learn the techniques of using inanimate utensils— brushes, pigments, textures, pianos, or guitars—to communicate the artistic idea, the dancer builds a personal instrument through a regimen of exercises, drills, and phrases. You become fully involved in stretching, reaching, folding, snapping, flouncing, diving, bobbing, and striving. Experiencing such an array of motion, the result of a progressive series of controlled, articulate movements, expands your horizon and ability to respond to, control and express a larger range of non-verbal impulses. This program, guided by your instructor, activates and trains the mind-body-spirit. It prepares you for transformation and freedom.

Dancers develop their abilities in a positive learning environment in which movements and phrases challenge them to grow. Techniques will be introduced in a non-competitive yet demanding manner. The accuracy of your movements and their expressiveness will be observed and commented upon because it is through your ability to perform movement that learning and achievement can be assessed. Effective music and an energetic pace are coordinated in each class to bring the dance experience into focus. It is inspiring and fun to dance and to achieve your movement goals. YOU are always the most important figure in the dance picture.

When dancing, you are the important figure.
Photo: Bruce Davis.

Making Learning Easy

Learning is accomplished through a pattern of thinking that is largely developed by each person individually. In your dance classes, be an active, aggressive learner. Use your body and mind fully; don't hold back. The information you experience must be integrated with how you best learn a subject. These differences in personal learning styles are characterized by how we rely upon the senses; how we respond to musical or visual cues; how we sort and retain new information; how we differentiate new information from previously learned concepts; and how we decide what is relevant to emphasize in our performance. Self-help tools aid us to remember and analyze verbal information, but little effort is made to guide us in seeing movement, understanding body language, or responding to stylistic gestures. Yet movement and gesture are natural ways of knowing and expressing.

During your dance studies, you will learn about the many artistic components of movement. Remember that focus, emphasis, and nuance are just as important as learning to shift weight, hold the body, and remember the sequence. Practical learning cues engage your mind. They increase your awareness of the artistic component, to help you to become aware of and remember these components. Read and understand these cues and replicate the movements. Only then will you begin to involve a personal perspective by drawing upon past experience and knowledge in a meaningful way. It's at this point that your rhythmic movements become dance.

In dance the learning process is not as simple as 1–2–3. Dance movement is a complex communicative and symbolic language. Learning dance vocabulary and its systematic arrangement into phrases is a sophisticated skill which isn't picked up in only a few classes.

Following are guidelines to perceiving and learning movement which will enhance your dancing:

1. See actively and attentively. Don't let your mind wander to subjects or plans that are irrelevant to the dance class. Although you're a part of a class situation, isolate yourself from outside thoughts that will hamper learning.
2. When presented with a new sequence, focus upon how and when the weight changes take place. Feel the rhythm of the step, the built-in signature of that movement.
3. Model your movements after your instructor as a sculptor might mold warm, moist clay to resemble the form being copied. It is the totality of the form, correctly proportioned, that you are imitating. See beyond the movement of the feet and legs. The arms, torso, facing direction, amount of force used, and focus are elements that are combined to create the look and expressive feeling of the step or phrase.
4. Vocalize internally to increase your perception of changes in direction, weight, level, and body isolations. Mirror the rhythmic signature of the step pattern with *doo-ops*, *dee-dahs*, or *bee-bops*. Great "scat" jazz singers like Bobby McFerrin and Ella Fitzgerald vocalize complex rhythm patterns in this way.

5. Develop a consistent approach for learning new techniques. A specific procedure for viewing and moving becomes an efficient, goal-directed method. In this way, you'll develop systematic guideposts by which to measure progress. You will know instinctively when clarification or feedback is needed to improve the rate and depth of learning.

6. Ask questions at the end of each lesson. Although teachers prefer that the flow of the lesson not be interrupted unnecessarily, they are usually eager to assist you personally after dismissing the rest of the class.

7. Mental practice in a quiet setting is a proven way to improve neuro-muscular responses. Between lessons, visualize yourself performing the movement sequence correctly. Hear both the accompaniment and the verbal cues, first in slow motion and then in proper tempo. Programming the mind and body to respond sequentially to those correct cues, you will become more aware of how and when you're moving.

8. Practice on a regular basis. This is fundamental to learning any highly coordinated mind-body activity. Note those movements that are posing a special challenge. Rehearse them to music that is similar in quality and tempo before your next lesson. Your active participation in learning by reviewing what was introduced in the lesson develops your readiness to progress.

9. Be alert to your group or ensemble. During your mental practices, think about performing with your group. Visualize the whole of the ensemble as well as your own part.

10. Finally, be open to the experience that your instructor has planned. Nothing can derail your best intentions more than self-criticism or unnecessary questioning about the class work. Gumming up the intricate neuro-motor switching system with a negative mental attitude restricts effective learning. It also robs you of the true enjoyment of expressive motion.

Structuring the Typical Jazz Class

Why is so much emphasis placed upon technical preparation for jazz dancing? Can't you just turn on your emotions with the music? Jazz dancers, like jazz musicians, need to develop a secure technique because it leads them to achieve a level of perfection as performers. Merce Cunningham, a leading figure in contemporary modern dance, wrote that movement: "appeals through the eye to the mind . . . the mind is not convinced by kinetics alone, the meaning must be clear. . . ."[1]

How does a typical jazz lesson unfold? What can you expect that is similar yet very different from other kinds of dance training?

Many classes are planned so that new techniques or step patterns are folded into previously learned sequences or short dance routines. This format provides you with a known stylistic structure upon which the new technique is learned. The style and specific skills that are to be mastered depend upon two separate yet interactive variables: the technical background and the personal style of your teacher.

Generally jazz classes begin with a warm-up to develop joint and muscle flexibility, abdominal, leg, and back strength, and rhythmic responsiveness. These simple sequences elevate the heart rate and lubricate the major joint and muscle structures of the body.

Janice LaPointe-Crump leads a class practicing side hip releases.
Photo: Denton Record Chronicle.

Many teachers will incorporate traditional sitting or standing modern dance exercises. Standing ballet barre exercises may be practiced either at a barre or in the center of the studio. An important part of the jazz technique class is studying isolated actions of parts of the body, at first singly and then coordinated with complete movement phrases. Jazz isolations consist of small, sharply accented actions of the head, shoulders, torso, and hips.

The hands are also particularly shaped in jazz dance. Gathering energy that relates directly to the intent of a movement, hands vibrate, slash, grab, and reach into space aggressively rather than passively putting a finishing touch on a movement.

Longer dance phrases are introduced that expand the scope of your technique and open your horizons to performing different rhythms and traditional jazz styles. After you've learned new step patterns, practiced turns and jumps, and reviewed other

Stretching is an important part of preparing the body to move.
Photo: TWU Dance Repertory Theatre.

previously learned materials, you may learn and perfect brief dances. These phrases may be designed so that you face various directions in the studio and take on a variety of characters or interpret different styles.

These first dances are usually developed around stylized walking patterns which have been seasoned by turns, falls, leaps, or high kicks, depending upon the abilities of the class. Because jazz embodies the expression of the soul through a personally derived technical discipline, there is really no classical pattern of how jazz must be learned.

Jazz dancers are assertive and forthright in the way they fully reveal human energy. Filling out the movement phrases with your own personal feeling is a vital part of the holistic jazz experience; after all, jazz is a hot, pulsating performing art form. Learn the dance routine or phrases well enough so that you can focus upon performance style, musical expression, spatial and weight/energy relationships. In this way you will come to communicate the dance idea fully.

Dancers practice battement tendu, a typical
ballet barre movement.
Photo: TWU Dance Repertory Theatre.

Hands create gesture and contribute to the
meaning of the movement.
Photo: Bruce Davis.

The final portion of a class consists of the cool-down. A relaxed and sustained stretching to blues or New Age music emphasizes a fluid stretching of the back, torso, legs, and arms. Completing the typical lesson, the cooling down process begins what a shower will complete.

End Note

1. Merce Cunningham and Jean Morrison-Brown, *Vision of Modern Dance,* (Princeton: University Press, 1979), p. 90.

3

The Jazz Connection:
The Basic Principles of Dance

At its simplest level, dancing can be thought of as a series of skips and turns, thrusts and drives, stops and starts. These primary actions are ordered into formal movement patterns or steps called *dance technique.* Technique tells the dancer how the body instrument is used. Through practice, the dancer learns to control and order movement in defined ways. These ways of moving make it possible for an audience to see what the dance is about and to appreciate and enjoy it.

As the dancer learns to execute the steps and traditional jazz movement patterns, technique is combined with expression. The dancer draws from feelings and kinesthetic perceptions to create a total dance portrait. In this way, a dancer learns to express different dance ideas or styles of jazz. The process consists of working and playing with how steps are executed. One approach is to vary the intensity of a dance phrase, from crescendo-like power to subtle flow. Another approach is to change the rhythmic accents of the steps from even to uneven. Ultimately the goal is to inject into a dance a personal flair or pizzazz. Think sassy!

Let's focus directly on you. Moving brilliantly is important, but never at the sacrifice of preserving the integrity of your body as a physical and passionate structure. Learning to move, pause, pounce, turn, jump, grab, fall, reach, bend, and slither must be done in a physically safe way. The result will be technical sureness and freedom. Take time to prepare your body carefully. Listen to your body. Practice correct form while having fun in your class. Apply these two imperatives, and you will succeed as a jazz dancer.

Much of what is practiced in your class has been designed to train groups of muscles located in the feet, legs, back, and abdomen. These major muscle groups need to react automatically and dynamically in order for you to become an articulate, powerful mover.

To attain this, you will practice some movements again and again so that correct mind and muscle patterning ensures safe action of the muscles and joints. Besides protecting you from a needless injury, a controlled, progressive approach builds confidence. Never attempt a technique that you're not ready to do. Your safety is valuable.

The place to begin your dance journey is in the studio, bursting with the energy of your teacher, the music, and you. Let the inspiration of this atmosphere empower you to vary and maximize your own sense of vitality. Observe how your fellow dancers perform during the lesson so that their enthusiasm rubs off on you.

In jazz dancing, rhythmic accents are frequently punctuated by specific isolated gestures. The rhythmic details of a step are related to the particular look or texture of a dance style. How the hips are held, whether the hands are gripped or fluttering, if the weight is lifted onto the toes or placed flat on the sole of the foot are all notable characteristics of dance movement. Look for them. These elements don't just add spice to your dancing, rather they are essential elements of the step pattern you're learning. Strive to see these details, then incorporate them into your performance. Technical accuracy is the target.

"Hors d'Oeuvre."
Photo: Les Ballets Jazz de Montréal.

Universal Principles of Dance Movement

Within the core of all jazz movement is a unique application of the universal principles governing motion. How the principles are applied forms a kind of "genetic code" for each step in the jazz vocabulary. These codes illustrate how jazz has become a unique, brilliant part of American culture. This chapter is devoted to examining several of these underlying principles of motion. Once you understand and apply them, the mystery cloaking new movement disappears.

Did you realize that general physical laws of motion are put into action whenever you jump, leap, run, or turn? Disguised by special gestures, dynamics of performance, and choreographic intent, the steps seem entirely new. Look through the disguise to understand how the body moves, so that you can learn the new steps quickly and more accurately. Then adjusting to new positions and different styles of jazz will become much easier.

Refer also to Chapter Eight. There you'll learn about dance movement analysis, rhythm, and how dance elements are linked to form particular jazz dance styles.

Motion is influenced by Sir Issac Newton's laws of inertia, gravity, and momentum. How you control your body in space is related also to your muscular strength and flexibility, the range of movement that your joints permit, and the efficiency with which you are able to move. Much of the time in any dance class is devoted to developing these three aspects of effective motion.

The body consists of a system of muscles which overlap each other in function. Coordinating their effort, the dancer develops the ability to move effortlessly and safely. We are most sensitive to the activity of the superficial muscles, those close to the surface of the skin. Visualize the muscles draped and stretched over the skeleton. In the following drawings of the front and back of the body, only the major muscles, ones that your teacher will refer to in class, have been labeled. Learn them so that you can begin to relate movement to muscular action.

In the thigh, for example, you should know that the dancer uses the sartorius, gracilis and adductors along with the quadriceps to lift or kick the leg forward. The hamstrings, located in the back of the thigh, must relax somewhat to permit the kick. When kicking to the back, the dancer contracts the gluteals, the back extensors, and the hamstrings while relaxing the quadriceps in order to execute a full kick.

That simply means that the dancer must both strengthen and stretch the muscles of the front and back thigh. Kicking to the front and back must be rehearsed until the dancer is able to control the coordinated efforts of the thigh muscles. Thus, the kick uses the full range of motion in the joints of the hip and lower spine.

The two vital muscular structures controlling your body in relation to the center of gravity are the iliopsoas and quadratus lumborum. These muscles, nestled deep in the pelvis, are connected to the lower lumbar spine and cross the front of the pelvis to attach to the upper part of the femur. The stability of the pelvis, influencing your balance, is affected by this group.

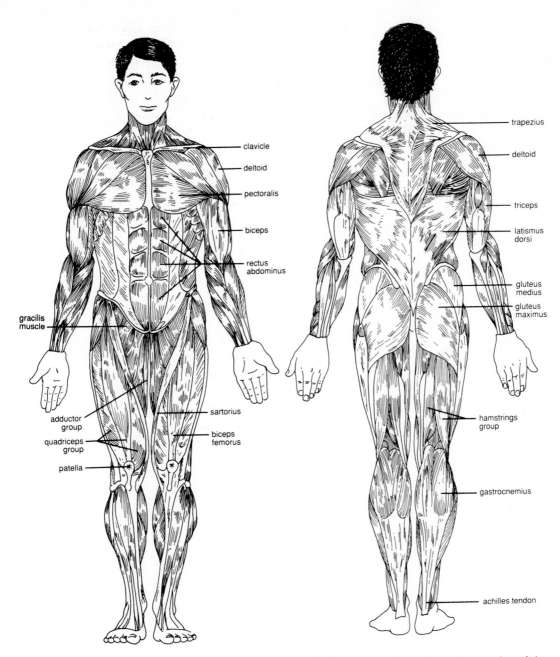

clavicle

deltoid

pectoralis

biceps

rectus
abdominus

gracilis
muscle

adductor
group

quadriceps
group

patella

sartorius

biceps
femorus

trapezius

deltoid

triceps

latismus
dorsi

gluteus
medius

gluteus
maximus

hamstrings
group

gastrocnemius

achilles tendon

The body moves by coordinating groups of muscles. This illustration shows the major muscles of the front and back parts of the body.

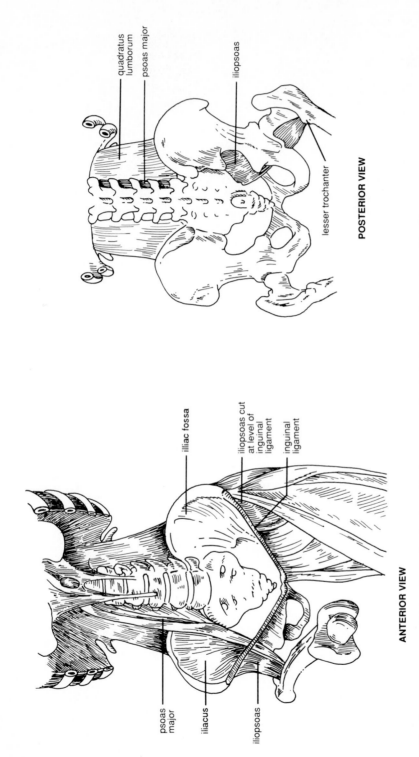

quadratus
lumborum

psoas major

iliopsoas

lesser trochanter

POSTERIOR VIEW

iliac fossa

iliopsoas cut
at level of
inguinal
ligament

inguinal
ligament

psoas
major

iliacus

iliopsoas

ANTERIOR VIEW

The iliopsoas group and quadratus lumborum play important roles in balancing the body, achieving high leg extensions above 90 degrees and aligning the legs with the torso.

Centering Integrates the Spine and Pelvis

Good alignment increases your sensitivity to how you are positioned in space during stillness and motion. Besides practicing improved postural habits, specific muscle strengthening is usually needed to control the pelvis, spine, and rib cage. Stretching, which will also improve range of motion, may be required in those muscles which tend to pull the torso from the center of gravity.

One way to assess your general strength and flexibility is to look at the curved lines of your body in relationship to your center line of gravity. The *center line of gravity* is an imaginary line running from the head through the center of the body into the floor, or base of support. *Centering* (balancing and harmonizing) the body means it adjusts around this line. Avoid over-correcting the position of the pelvis to improve a sense of center. When the weight of the body is balanced efficiently through the skeleton and joints, you will feel a catlike ease and readiness to move. Never jar or yank muscles and

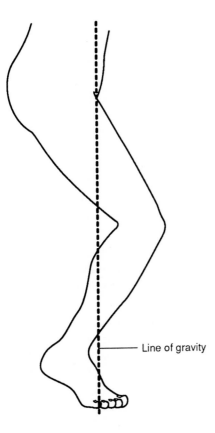

— Line of gravity

No matter what position you are in, the center line of gravity must fall directly in front of the ankle.

joints in order to maintain control or to move quickly or strongly. Roughly treating your instrument is traumatic. Building up traumas to the ligaments and cartilage of the joints and to the fibers of the muscles may result in later injuries.

Centering is a dynamic, efficient readiness that results from applying alignment principles to your own body. Following are tips to maintain good posture which contribute to centering. Apply them daily and you will find that when engaged correctly your muscles and joints will move powerfully yet easily.

Head Tilt the chin slightly upward. Feel a warm cushion at the base of the neck, under the ears; relax the neck.

Shoulders Envision the shoulders as a yoke that is draped over the top of the rib cage. The edges of the shoulders reach sideward, away from the center or sternum. Your upper back is widened with the shoulder blades, or scapulae, and held downward.

Rib Cage The very top of the sternum, where the clavicles meet, is lifted easily as though you were showing off a medallion. When exhaling, the upper part of the rib cage remains elevated. The front of the ribs never juts upward or forward, Instead, the ribs float easily on top of the pelvis. Separate the back of the ribs from the back of the pelvis, and allow them to slide upward when inhaling. Exhale smoothly without sinking in to the lower back.

Breath The breath cycle plays an important role in dancing. Breathing is coordinated with the movements to increase articulation and ensure a controlled quality. Controlled breathing synchronizes use of the torso and pelvic floor. Instead of lifting and lowering the rib cage or allowing the abdomen to protrude and contract as we usually do, dancers coordinate the opening and closing of the ribs along with a widening of the middle back area and a lifting and lowering of the diaphragm. Sense an easy floating at the base of the neck. If the neck is tense, natural breath control is hampered. Exhale thoroughly. Empty the lungs, and they will fill naturally.

Try this simple exercise: Yawn deeply two to three times, rolling the head gently from side-to-side. Practice slow head rolls to increase the flexibility and fluid motion in the neck and upper back, vital to effective breathing.

Pelvis The center of gravity is located slightly above the pelvis (higher in men than in women). Therefore, the pelvic girdle is the most important structure in the development of an agile, controlled dancer. Your goal is to develop control by integrating the lower abdominals with the deep iliopsoas muscles. These in turn are synchronized with the hip rotators and gluteal muscles (the buttocks). The lower back lengthens while a slight contraction of the abdominals lifts the weight up and over the feet. Many of us spend too much of the day seated, thighs flexed and buttocks relaxed. Toning work is required to gain that dynamic lift in the lower abdominal region and a complementary lengthening in the lower back.

Legs When standing, imagine hanging from a bar. Your thighs dangle from the pelvis increasing the feeling of length at the base of the sacroiliac joint (pelvis) and coccyx (tailbone). Since the legs are joined to the pelvis at a point close to the center line of the body, the area in front of the hip elongates also. Can you maintain these sensations? The more you can, the freer your range of motion at the hip joint.

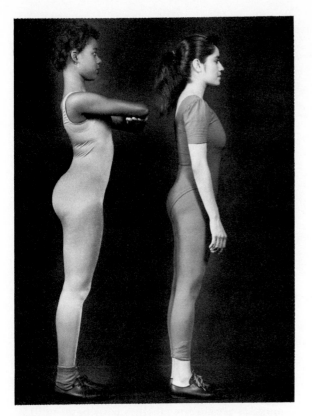

Incorrect (L) and correct (R) body alignment. Notice how the rib cage and lower back are held in each dancer. To aid in correct rib cage placement, think of supporting a shelf from the lower ribs.
Photo: Bruce Davis.

Try this mild stretch:

Extend and flatten the back of the pelvis and the front of the hip joint. Then reach your arms and legs in opposite directions. Don't arch your back.

Stretch the right arm and leg away from your center without arching the back. Think of yourself as a straight laser beam.
Photo: Bruce Davis.

Draw the heel along the floor to flex the knee; keep the pelvis stable.
Photo: Bruce Davis.

Now bend one knee keeping the foot flat on the floor. Slide that foot out slowly until the knee is extended, the foot pointed. The back of the thigh (hamstrings) feels weighted, almost drawn down under the floor. Slowly bend the knee drawing the foot up returning to the starting position. Don't arch the lower back during the leg movement. How does the pelvis react as the abdominal muscles are hollowed? It is your base; hold it still. Repeat eight times with each leg until the thigh is smoothly aligned with the pelvis.

Opposition and Parallel Use of the Body

Opposition is demonstrated when you walk. The arms naturally swing in opposition to the leading foot in a functional not decorative manner. Counterbalancing the activity of the torso, these movements guarantee smooth and controlled motion.

Try this: Walk forward, allowing the arms to react freely. How do the arms respond to the body's motion when you cease controlling them? The shoulders and shoulder blades (*scapulae*) slide easily back and forth resulting in a slight swinging action. Repeat with both arms crossed over your chest or extended overhead. Awkward isn't it? As though fighting an invisible force, your body has lost its smooth flow through space.

Many jazz phrases are based upon walking patterns. The arm positions or gestures used are usually designed in opposition to the stepping foot in order to make shifting weight easier. Anticipating this will make your learning process easier.

Since surprise and accent are stressed in jazz dancing, gestures or movements that correspond to the center of weight are interspersed into a sequence or phrase. These parallel actions create a robust asymmetrical force. Don't let this brief change to parallel arms throw you off balance. Simply shift your weight more deeply over the supporting leg to compensate for this sudden change in emphasis and effort.

Jazz lunge with opposition arms.
Photo: Bruce Davis.

Jazz lunge with parallel arms.
Photo: Bruce Davis.

Parallel Use of Arms is exciting because of the spontaneous, syncopated use of the body. Because too much opposition results in monotony and predictability, jazz dancers shift from opposition to parallel. Yet, moving abruptly and precisely to a new facing direction or spinning on one foot and then dropping suddenly to the floor requires a shift from a state of balance to one of imbalance. Such quick changes require confidence in being off center and slightly out of control.

Try this: Cross your right foot in back of the left and execute a one-half pivot to face the opposite wall. You probably pulled your right shoulder back as you turned your head in that direction. Next, walk in a large clockwise circle. Did you notice how you leaned automatically into the center of the circle? In both exercises, your motion paralleled the direction of the movement. Dancing actually amplifies natural reactions to spatial forces. To enhance learning, become aware of these natural compensations for the external forces acting on the body.

Let's trick the body. Repeat both exercises except this time hold your arms and shoulders in opposition to the direction of the pivot. Avoid favoring the direction of the circular walk. Don't compensate or lean into the direction of the turn or circle. Isn't that awkward?

Lifting out of the floor brings the dancer's weight out of the base of support.
Photo: Bruce Davis.

This dancer clearly supports the side leg extension through the lifted pelvis. The character of the movement is defined by clear details of hands and feet.
Photo: Jennifer Collins. TWU Dance Repertory Theatre.

Shifting Weight

To shift weight smoothly, dancers control where the center of weight falls through the foot. Anatomically, weight is transferred onto the supporting foot slightly ahead of the ankle joint. This is fine for stable, vertical positions, but the dancer, like the athlete, must be poised for quick action. Shifting, starting, and stopping are simple yet vital components of expert dancing.

Lifting out of the floor through engaged abdominals, tightened gluteals (buttocks), and lifted adductor and hamstring muscles (the inner and back of the thigh), your weight is held over the metatarsal bones of the foot, the mid-arch area. You are balanced over the three weight-bearing points of the foot: the heel, great toe, and fifth toe. To perform a quick flurry of movement, your weight shifts immediately onto the balls of the feet without rolling inward on the ankle, called *pronation,* or outward, called *supination,* or sickling.

Since the correct use of the feet (to change direction, to propel the body through space, and to recover from a leap) is imperative, a considerable amount of class time is devoted to correct foot alignment, flexibility, and strengthening.

Let's explore your range of motion in the ankle and foot. Rise slowly and smoothly, lifting your heels as high as they can go. Notice the forward and upward movement of the body as it is carried up over the metatarsal arches of the feet. The toes must lie almost flat. If they begin to curl under, lower your heels and repeat until the toes remain flat.

The center line of gravity runs in front of the ankle through the lifted arch of the dancer's foot.
Artist: Craig Turski.

Pressing through the instep stretches the arches.
Photo: Jennifer Collins.

How high did you rise? Look in a mirror and compare the position of your feet and ankles with the figure below. Ideally, the ankle should form a vertical line to the metatarsals. If the ankle is behind that line, the muscles of the calf and the joints of the foot strain when you rise off the floor to three-quarter point or to jump. Practice the foot stretching exercises taught in class at least three times per week until your range of motion in the ankle and foot improves.

Rise to relevé in fifth position by pressing into the floor as you lift the heels.
Photo: Jennifer Collins.

The dancer pulls the thigh into her hip as the gesture arm reaches in opposition to create a powerful dance image.
Photo: Jennifer Collins. TWU Dance Repertory Theatre.

All three previously described principles of movement are applied in a spinning turn. You begin by *shifting your weight* forward to maximize balance and control. There is a moment of stability to prepare for the turn with an *oppositional* arm gesture. The burst of energy in the turn occurs by closing the arms quickly into a fixed shape. Thus, *parallel* force is used. Stability is an important part of turning. Therefore, momentum is generated in a controlled way by the second arm closing swiftly to meet the first arm. This arm returns to an open position (in opposition to the direction of the turn) as the turn concludes, readying your transition to the next movement.

Opposition of Forces

Pressing into the floor yet extending the joints away from gravity provides dynamic resilience for maintaining balance no matter how tilted the body is off a direct vertical line. We have talked about the need to lengthen the spine along its vertical axis while suspending the rib cage above the pelvis. Kinesthetically, sense a reaching of the legs and feet away from the center line of gravity, or pelvic girdle, as you kick, jump, or take a step.

When jumping, the dancer thrusts against the force of gravity.
Photo: Bruce Davis.

Press into the floor to extend the torso and project the body in the opposite direction.
Photo: Bruce Davis.

The dancer does not move passively in space. On the contrary, gravity is counteracted any time the center of gravity is lowered. Two examples are bending the knees in a *plié* or recovering from a jump. Gravity is resisted by involving the anti-gravity muscles (the gluteals, hamstrings, and adductors) to prevent a real fall. No matter how spontaneous a dance fall appears or how light the dancer seems to float, a dancer never submits entirely to gravity. This invites injury. Yet, the jazz dancer is unique in the way gravity is manipulated. Instead of appearing effortless like a ballet dancer, a jazz dancer moves with and against gravity with dynamic tension. You can almost see these natural forces.

Action and reaction are seen easily in a *relevé* (rising up on the toes) or in a jump. Pushing downward sharply into the floor, maximum thrust results when the body remains organized around the center line of gravity. The body is propelled into dynamic balance regardless of the shape created.

This primary concept of physics is applied again in the *arabesque, jazz lay-out,* and supported positions. (See Chapter Five for descriptions of these poses.) In these more advanced poses, you reach the torso, head, and arms in a direction opposite to the pelvis and gesture leg. Like cables supporting a suspension bridge, your center of gravity isn't left hanging but is suspended or braced between oppositional energy force fields.

Focus and Expression

Nothing is more important to the polished appearance of a movement than integrating your internal and external focus. The ability to direct mind, body, and spirit to heighten a particular moment which transcends time and place is the dancer's quest. Gesture,

External focus directs attention to a particular direction in space.
Photo: Jennifer Collins. TWU Dance Repertory Theatre.

focus, and facial attitude are primary tools of the dance expression. It's not only *what* you say but *how* you say it that ensures good communication to an audience. Applying these tools of expression in your own dancing and observing this in others are skills that can be applied outside the studio to everyday living.

External focus is the easily observed surface of movement. Look intently at a movement to see the contours of the body, the step pattern, and its placement in space in relation to the music. The direction you are looking to and the lines the body makes contribute to external focus.

Internal focus refers to the kinesthetic and emotional motivation which are equally important to the ultimate meaning of a movement. Your personal image is meaningful because it tells the audience why you are moving in a particular way. The audience can almost feel the extremely taut arm or the exhilarating power in a dramatic thrust.

The mirror is used when learning to focus effectively and to punctuate movement dynamically. As you look closely in the mirror, note what the movement looks like. Absorb the muscular tension and the emotional sense of it. Study the demonstrated images so that you become more accurate in replicating the instructor's steps with a similar range of energy and space.

Next, begin to explore a range of personal inner images that are suggested by the movements. Think of metaphors which can relate directly to the content of the movement: its style, rhythm, force, space, tempo, or flow.

The painter Ben Shahn thinks that using images helps us to become vibrant, effective communicators. For him, the creating of personal allegories are an important part of being artistic. From the moment at which a painter (or anyone) begins to express oneself, Shahn advises that "he must become acutely sensitive to the feel, the textures, the light, the relationships which arise before him."[1] In the case of jazz dance, the contrasts in size, energy, space, phrasing, style, and musical tempo are important cues to that inner voice, called the *internal focus*. Small, tight isolated steps might be likened to flicking threads off of a sweater or playing a video game. Large, boisterous jumps and pinwheellike turns might remind one of a water skier jumping a wake or a barrel racer leaning with the horse around a curve.

Jazz Dance as an Art Form

The linking of emotional release, movement, and sound are particularly clear in jazz dancing. In a purely physical way, jazz dance is an art form that relies upon the syncopation and beat of the music, masked by few compositional conventions. The jazz dancer lingers with an idea and a style of movement as they merge with a particular theme in the music—blues to new age, hard driving rock to bouncy disco, flippant Latin reggae to big band swing. Never separated from human expressiveness, jazz responds to the deepest roots of language and to our hopes and fears. Never passive, jazz movements resonate with the rich, passionate echoes of life.

Added to this intense interplay is an atmosphere charged with strong dance technique and *flash* personal spirit. Each jazz dance should be colorful, unique, and spectacular. "It's groovy," writes *Newsweek* columnist Hubert Saal. "Body English is an

Internal focus gives an introspective form to "Fusion." Jazzdance: The Danny Buraczeski Dance Company.
Photo: Bob Brody.

eloquent language all its own."[2] Such is the diversity of jazz dance that it can't be tied to any one style or method. Think of choreographers like Bob Fosse, Katherine Dunham, Alvin Ailey, Paula Abdul, Fred Astaire, and Michael Jackson. They are all very different. Each has worked from a creative intention, adding to the jazz tradition. They paved the way for the next generation to think in freshly innovative dance terms rather than to reproduce hackneyed step patterns from the past.

Dance is a unique art form because the ideas and images you perceive reside in the motion itself. They cannot be represented in any other medium. Many choreographers think of their work as an expression of dance ideas. For Jerome Robbins, choreographer of *West Side Story,* dance communicates to "the audience through the physical expression of movement and gesture." For him "language symbols gave way to dance images."[3]

Dancers enjoy the sensuous joy of motion in "Hors d'Oeuvre." Les Ballets Jazz de Montréal.
Photo: Ian Westbury.

The late choreographer, Michael Bennett, contended that the best dance entertainment arises from a concept and then is developed through themes and finally transformed into actual steps. His *A Chorus Line* and *Dreamgirls* have made lasting impressions on the development of theater dancing. ''My approach to everything in dancing,'' said Bennett, ''is not in the step kick, step kick, back, change, step kick. . . .What I want to do is to make the movement give a psychological insight into a character, to advance the story and make a point quickly.''[4]

Think about these points when you are watching a performance. See *how* a movement is performed and think about what you're being led to sense about a dance. Avoid making quick decisions about liking or not liking what you see. Instead, look for design elements, linkages between the movement and the music and the movement and the dance idea. These elements are brought together in the following exercise.

Try this: Look at your hand as it reaches away from you. Grab at something, then snatch that hand strongly into your chest. Perform the phrase abruptly six times.

What are some images that this highly charged action brings to mind? How about a whip, or an angry response to a nasty remark? Repeat the pattern very slowly. Let the hand and arm glide forward effortlessly. How did you respond to the change in speed? Did you feel like floating in a wave pool or as though you were disconnected from your muscles? Which way was more pleasing? Or invigorating?

As you learn various jazz steps and patterns, always appreciate your natural rhythmic style and preferences. Each movement portrays different attributes of motion as space, time, energy, and flow. You can personalize your dance experiences by developing the ability to fill a movement with an image that relates to these attributes. In this way the audience will be encouraged to perceive a similar idea or memory from seeing *you dance*.

End Notes

1. Ben Shahn, *The Shape of Content,* (Cambridge, MA: Harvard University Press, 1957), pp. 48–49.
2. Richard Kislan, *Hoofing on Broadway,* (New York, NY: Prentice-Hall Press, 1987), pp. 94.
3. Ibid., p. 95.
4. Ibid., p. 117.

4

Let's Get Moving:
Designing Your Warm-Up

Now that you're beginning to know about the world of jazz dance, let's think about those characteristics which make this kind of dancing unique. As a performance art, jazz unlocks a kinetic-sensual relationship with life. It correlates emotions and psychological attitudes with the pathways of non-verbal expression. Since jazz dance represents active and assertive characteristics, the jazz dancer reveals something of the inner self through her or his dancing.

"Out of the Blues," Jazzdance: The Danny Buraczeski Dance Company.
Photo: Robin Holland.

Wellness as Physical and Spiritual Fitness

Ben Vereen, who starred in *Pippin* and was featured in the film, *All That Jazz,* knows the spiritual gift that his dancing gives him. Over the years, a grinding performance and film schedule robbed him of that vital part of his life. Vereen became consumed by career stress and the loss of friends and family. He ignored the natural stress reduction that can occur when unhealthy levels of tension are redirected by expressing them in movement.

The emotions and tensions inherent in a high tech life-style like Vereen's almost ended a promising career. What he had to recognize was the *substance* of dance and the deep spirit that had gone unnourished. Once he returned to the dance studio, Vereen began to fully understand the role of dance in his life. "Now I appreciate it," he said. "To move through space is a spiritual thing. There's something about dancing that keeps you young forever."[1]

Speaking retrospectively, what he had to offer was unique. "I worked so hard to be accomplished," he explained. "I had the enthusiasm and the love for it, and that weighed out."[2] What does Vereen's enthusiasm and love for dancing mean to you? Dance is a brilliant performance art. Jazz in particular allows you to burst forth in energetic, and spatially and rhythmically precise ways. Jazz contributes to a healthy life-style in another way. It's a means of expressing yourself personally and of connecting your inner spirit with your outer physical being.

Why is the dance class a more complete path to healthful living than other forms of fitness or wellness activities? Jazz is a form of dance involving the realms of human interaction. The intellectual, physical, emotional, aesthetic, and spiritual are joined in an integrated mind-body experience. Cognition and intuition are linked.

Optimum personal benefits are possible whenever you experience positive as well as challenging activities. Designed by your instructor, the dance lesson integrates thought, feeling, and action in movement. The exercises and dance sequences will develop specific movement abilities and enhance your sensitivity to space, time, and energy. Through this process, you will come to admire your own unique world view. Good physical and mental health occurs from being *present,* rather than a bystander, in your life.

The inner and outer experiences of life are merged in non-verbal communication. The very act of expressing your inner self in this highly rhythmical and expressionistic dance form is an act of empowerment. The results are many: improved self-image; increased emotional well-being; enhanced use of gestural interplay; improved physical strength and flexibility (*anaerobic* fitness); increased heart-lung capacity (*aerobic* fitness); and more. Assuming authority over everyday problems and becoming sensitive to the significance of living will enrich the quality and substance of your life.

Dance is not a mindless act! You are thinking about the body's movements, directing them consciously as you explore their potential. Going beyond the body's actions, you will begin to involve life experiences and attitudes in your movement. The first step is to

The mind as well as the body is involved in learning to dance.
Photo: TWU Dance Repertory Theatre.

become acquainted with the movement and inflection that you naturally do. How do you become more aware of the body during motion? In the beginning, it may be difficult to sense the many aspects of a movement and interpret them simultaneously. Over time you will improve your ability to perceive the cooperation between the muscles and joints during stillness and motion. Active listening to your body improves postural and movement habits.

Dancers work diligently to sense the changing relationship and action of muscles and joints in relation to time and space. A muscle responding briskly, in a fraction of a second, feels quite different from the same muscle gliding in a light, sustained manner. A small, tight movement of the hand is distinctive from an expansive movement involving the arm.

The remainder of this chapter is devoted to another stage in developing the dancer: personally preparing for the jazz lesson, called the *warm-up*.

"The 40's" by Lou Conté.
Kitty Skillman Hilsabeck Hubbard Street Dance Company.
Photo: Jennifer Girard.

The Values of Warming Up

A patterned warm-up routine establishes a ritual in which you increasingly concentrate upon mind-body sensitivity while developing strength, flexibility, and coordination. The repetitive nature of warm-ups allows you to focus directly upon *how* rather than *what* you are doing. Distracting outside thoughts are eliminated. Concentration, also called *mental presence,* plays an important role in the physical readiness of the neuro-musculo-skeletal systems. Therefore, good study habits in dance should be acquired early on to ensure a positive disciplined mode of working so that your movement goals may be accomplished. By establishing such habits, you are also assuming responsibility for yourself.

A good warm-up is more than a physical act. It is a way of attending to and focusing upon how the mind and body are coordinating their various functions. Learn to designate a movement goal, then free the mind and body to solve the problem in its own way. While the body progresses through this process, freely associate the impulse to move with knowing that the body can and will find its solution. Begin to apply the essential principles of dynamic balancing during stillness and motion. A multitude of physical responses coordinate to align the segments of the body and prepares them for motion. The result is efficient and effective postural habits and your best of physical performance.

Preventing injuries is very important. The following series of controlled, easy movements makes use of the best knowledge about the functioning of the body. We know that properly warming up protects the body from muscle strains and joint tightness. Over time, failure to warm up sufficiently may weaken joint and bone structures, leading to chronic knee, foot, and lower back problems.

Following is a list of the most notable benefits from performing a progressive warm-up program prior to vigorous dance classes or rehearsals:

1. The heart rate elevates somewhat to route blood to muscles and joints.
2. The major postural muscles, those located in the back, buttocks, thighs, calves, and shoulder girdle are lengthened.
3. The abdomen and waist area is narrowed and lifted.
4. The principal joint areas of the shoulder, spine, pelvis, knees, ankles, and feet become pliant.
5. The mind and body connect to achieve postural centering.
6. The major segments of the torso are lifted above the body's center of gravity.
7. The abdominal muscles are strengthened.
8. Finally, the temperature of the body is raised about one to two degrees to a point which is optimum for effective neuro-muscular responding.

Let us first think about how the warm-up exercises affect your body. Review the illustrations in Chapter Three so that you'll be ready to explore what occurs to a body part when the muscles contract. Remember, a muscle contracts to shorten or flex the joint it crosses. It stretches or elongates to extend the joint only by the contraction of an opposing muscle, not by its own action. Therefore, to perform a high forward kick, which requires strong quadriceps action, the gluteals and hamstrings must be pliant enough to stretch. If they are tight, the kick will be low and stiff. The pelvis will tilt, disturbing good posture and sacrificing balance.

Although never fully releasing a contraction, the muscle relaxes somewhat in order to be stretched. If it relaxed entirely, you would lose control over that body part, and movement would have a spastic quality. Rarely does only one muscle move a single body part. Therefore, it takes repeated practice of a movement for your muscles to learn to coordinate with one another, responding harmoniously to produce accurate, coordinated motion.

Selected Warm-Up Exercises

The following exercises are grouped by standing and floor positions. You may do either one or the other series since the body zones used are similar. You may select some exercises from each category. Sit-ups and push-ups, however, must always be included.

Dancers learn to perform the same movement on different levels, to create a tight angular image.
Dance: Stop Company.
Photo: Denny Cohen.

References are made to basic foot and arm positions and movements, like demi plié. If you are not familiar with a term, refer to Chapter Five for a description and explanation of these ballet movements before completing the exercises.

Standing Exercises

Begin all standing exercises in good posture with lifted abdominals. While the descriptions emphasize particular zones of the body, involve the whole body in reaching, bending, lengthening, contracting, and circling actions.

Reaching Pulses

Begin by standing in a natural first position. Alternate arm reaches overhead pulling upward strongly through the entire side of the body. Contrast it with an oppositional pull down into the floor with the other side. Repeat 8 times.

Bend your torso to the right, left arm curved overhead. Pulse gently, lifting the waist up and over the pelvis with each pulse. Shoulders are pressed downward. Repeat 8 times.

Demi plié while circling the arms down and around to the left side. Take 8 counts. Repeat the whole sequence.

Reaching pulses.
Photo: Bruce Davis.

Spine Ripples

Begin by standing in a natural first position. Demi plié and release the spine into a high arch; pull your elbows behind the torso, palms facing upward; look upward to a high diagonal. Do not overly arch the back or put pressure on the lower spine. Look downward while drawing the torso into a deep overcurve so that hands lightly brush the floor, as though you were hanging over a bar. Engage the abdominals in a strong upward lift.

Extend the legs, balancing some weight on the hands, to stretch the hamstrings and gluteals. Hold the pelvis over the forefoot area, not on the heels. If there is any discomfort in the back of the knees, flex them slightly to release the strain. Demi plié lifting up the back of the pelvis. Repeat the knee extension, then demi plié while carefully uncurling the spine and extending the knees to return to a lifted, vertical position.

Do the complete sequence 4 times in natural first position; then repeat it in turned out second position.

Spine Ripples. Begin all
exercises with lifted yet light
posture. Don't tighten the
back of the neck.
Photo: Bruce Davis.

Release the spine with
abdominals strongly lifted.
Photo: Bruce Davis.

Impulse forward into an
overcurve.
Photo: Bruce Davis.

Lengthen the knees, lifting
the hamstrings and
abdominals.
Photo: Bruce Davis.

Maintain a defined shape as
you uncurl to standing
position.

Impulse through the spine to
roll up sequentially.
Photo: Bruce Davis.

The Merry-Go-Round

Increases your sensitivity to speed. Notice how the feel of the movement changes with the increased tempo. Begin by standing in natural second position (an open stance, feet about 8–10 inches apart). Starting with your head, circle smoothly and continuously each listed body part. The progression includes the head, shoulders, elbows, full arm, wrists, rib cage, hip, and feet. Impulse each circle distinctly, but avoid ballistic thrusting actions. Begin with 8 counts for each circle. Repeat it to the left. Repeat the complete cycle again with 4 counts per circle. Repeat the cycle a third time, with 2 counts per body part. As the time is reduced, how does your sense of time, space, and energy vary?

Rocket Orbits

To work the waist in a two dimensional plane. Begin in a natural second position. Open the arms through second position and reach overhead. Clasp the right wrist with the left hand, without elevating the shoulders. Circle the torso to the left by pulling the right wrist with the left hand. Maintain a lifted center and engaged abdominals.

Continue to circle slowly, reaching to the far edges of a large imaginary spherical orbit. Let the action flow downward so that the hands brush the floor lightly and continue around to a vertical position. Repeat 4 times to each side.

1. *Merry-Go-Round.* Circle the head easily on an impulse.
   Photo: Bruce Davis.

2. Enjoy feeling how the torso reacts to the impulse of the shoulder circle.
   Photo: Bruce Davis.

3. Continue with an elbow circle.
   Photo: Bruce Davis.

4. Broaden the action into a full arm circle.
Photo: Bruce Davis.

5. Open the arms to better feel the rib circling movement.
Photo: Bruce Davis.

6. Low and funky, impulse into a large hip circle. It's fun to let the body respond freely.
Photo: Bruce Davis.

1. Begin the rocket orbit exercise by standing in second position.
   Photo: Bruce Davis.

2. Curve upward and over as deeply as possible. Don't sag into the supporting hip.
   Photo: Bruce Davis.

3. Grasp wrist and pull the torso into a deep side bend.
   Photo: Bruce Davis.

4. Continue to circle to an upright position.
   Photo: Bruce Davis.

1. Slide rib cage to the right to begin pulsing rocket orbits.
   Photo: Bruce Davis.

2. Circle over to the left, shifting your weight onto the left foot.
   Photo: Bruce Davis.

Pulsing Rocket Orbits

Begin in an easy second position; arms reaching sideward. Slide your rib cage smoothly to the right without twisting or dropping into the hip. Lift the right arm. Bend to the left, circling arms overhead. Demi plié during the circle carrying the torso down around to the other side. Extend the knees and continue to circle the right arm overhead to end in the starting position. Repeat 4 times, alternating sides.

Tabletop Releases

To deeply stretch legs and hips. Begin in an easy second position with the arms open in second position. Hinge the torso forward at the hip joint, engaging the abdominals in a strong upward lift. On this plane, maintain a lengthened head and neck alignment while reaching the arms sideward from the body's center. Don't flex the hips beyond a 90 degree angle. (See Chapter Six for a description of hinges.) Demi plié in this position.

3. Continue the orbit, lifting the abdominals as the torso circles.
Photo: Bruce Davis.

4. Reach the left arm to a high diagonal as you recover back to second position.
Photo: Bruce Davis.

Beginning with a strong abdominal contraction, extend your knees and form a concave shape with the torso. Pull upward strongly under the rib cage. (See Chapter Five for an explanation of contractions.)

Release the contraction while extending to a tabletop position. Lower in a demi plié. Repeat these movements 3 times.

Now dive slowly downward while the knees extend. Grasp your calves in this extreme upside down position; your weight is centered over the forefoot, not the heel. Sustain the stretch for 8 counts. Return the torso to a forward tabletop position without hyperextending the lower or lumbar spine. Imagine a bowling ball pressing against your abdomen, as you uncurl the back and extend the pelvis to vertical. Repeat 2 times.

For a variation, twist so that you are doing the tabletop and the releases to a forward diagonal. The feet, legs, and pelvis are held straight forward.

1. Tabletop releases. Begin in second position, ribs held in and lifted.
   Photo: Bruce Davis.

2. Lift the abdominals and lengthen the neck parallel to the floor.
   Photo: Bruce Davis.

3. Plié holding the tabletop position.
   Photo: Bruce Davis.

4. Contract strongly to change the spine into a deep curve.
   Photo: Bruce Davis.

5. Dive downward strongly, pressing the pelvic center forward over the feet.
   Photo: Bruce Davis.

Weighted Leg Swings

To prepare you for straight and fan kicks. All swings are performed outward away from the axis point to create freer motion around the hip joint.

Stand in an easy first position, arms in second with the left leg extending backward. Swing the left leg forward strongly and simultaneously swing the right arm forward to counterbalance the gesture leg. Reverse the arm and leg swing, creating a forward-backward pendulum effect. Look directly forward to assist the dynamic balancing process. Initiate each leg swing from the inner thigh muscles (the adductors), and extend your foot as it releases from the floor. Do this movement with a flexed working knee (called *attitude*) 8 times on each leg. Repeat the sequence using an extended working leg, called *grand battement en clôche*.

Prances

To warm the joints of the foot and strengthen the muscles of the arch. Begin by standing in a parallel first position with your weight forward over the metatarsals. Abruptly flex one knee, extending sequentially the ankle, instep, and toes so that the foot points downward. In reverse order, lower the foot to the floor in first position. Simultaneously repeat with the other foot. Repeat 16 times at a rapid pace.

Weighted Leg Swings. Sweep the leg downward brushing through first position. Let the momentum lift the thigh with the opposite arm swinging forward.
Photo: Bruce Davis.

Extend the working leg to increase the volume of the swing and to challenge your balance.
Photo: Bruce Davis.

Feet Beats. Stretch the feet fully during prances. Think light and buoyant.
Photo: Bruce Davis.

Floor Exercises

Exercising in seated or laying positions allows you to concentrate more easily upon alignment so that you can move the body more accurately and distinctly. Avoid relaxing the torso. A lifted center is always important.

Breathelizer

Begin seated cross-legged in a butterfly sit with abdominals elevated. You should achieve an almost completely vertical spine. Hold your arms comfortably, wrists laying across the knees.

Exhale sharply, blowing the air out of your mouth engaging the abdominals and the diaphragm area. On this exhale, curve the spine forward. The tailbone (coccyx) is connected to the floor while you inhale and elongate the spine to a forward diagonal hinge. Initiate the lift from the abdominal muscles. Gradually open your arms to second position. Extend to a vertical line with the arms progressing upward to fifth position: Lift and lengthen the back and waist without elevating the shoulders or thrusting the rib cage forward.

In the second part of this exercise, not illustrated extend your legs forward, straightening the knees and extending the feet. Now inhale and elevate the sternum looking upward. This rather small arching of the spine is called a *high back release*.

Hinge forward at the hips and exhale, elongating the spine while reaching forward over the thighs. The hamstrings and gluteals are stretched by reaching beyond your feet with the knees straight and heels on the floor. Hold for 8 counts.

1. *Breathelizer*. Exhale sharply to press the ribs upward and back in a strong contraction.
Photo: Bruce Davis.

2. Deepen the movement, carrying the spine forward.
Photo: Bruce Davis.

3. Pitch forward in a hinge, yet keep the coccyx connected to the floor.
Photo: Bruce Davis.

4. Lengthen the spine sequentially to achieve a strong diagonal hinge line.
Photo: Bruce Davis.

The *high back release.* A small movement of the upper spine with an elevated focus.
Photo: Bruce Davis.

Grasp the top of the toes, pulling them back to flex the ankle. Don't lift the heels off the floor since the knees may hyper-extend. Uncurl the spine back to a vertical, drawing your legs into the butterfly position with the opposite foot on top. You are ready to repeat the entire sequence.

Thigh Releases

To limber the strong, usually tight quadriceps (front of the thigh) and the hip socket region. Begin seated in the swastika position, right leg front. Each thigh approaches a 90 degree angle. Lean diagonally onto the right hand and reach the left arm across to grasp the right knee. Hold for 30 seconds.

Then sweep the knee forward and upward, maintaining flexion, into a deep hinging of the left hip socket, called *creasing.* The left arm, moving parallel to this movement, swings forward with the leg. Reverse the action, sweeping the leg down and back to the original position. As you begin to feel the weight of the thigh, sense its natural connection through the hip to the back of the pelvis into the lumbar spine. Repeat for 8 sweeps. Change sides and repeat the complete sequence.

Fourth position thigh stretches improve movements like splits and grand jeté.
Photo: Bruce Davis.

Begin thigh creases in fourth position, with weight lifted out of the supporting hip.
Photo: Bruce Davis.

Sweep the back leg forward, sensing the support in the working hip joint.
Photo: Bruce Davis.

Advanced movements, like the Swedish Fall,
require strong arms, back, and abdominals to
maintain the impact of this dramatic movement.
Photo: Bruce Davis.

Sit-Ups

Sit-Ups involve abdominal not postural muscles. They function little during everyday activity, so they can become chronically weak and flabby. Nevertheless, they are a keystone system of muscles (including the deep pelvic iliopsoas and quadratus lumborum) whose strength and resiliency safeguards the vulnerable, flexible lumbar spine. Their action enables the body's center of balance and weight to be shifted and supported with fine precision. Consequently, everyone should follow a strengthening program.

The following exercises progress in difficulty. Don't perform movements beyond your ability to maintain correct form. Begin with 8 repetitions, then work up to at least 50. Select moderate tempo music and maintain a steady pace. Consistency, not spurts of movement, is the key to improving the overall strength and stamina of these muscles.

To ensure safe muscle use, exhale strongly as you curl the head, neck, and torso upward. Inhale as the torso lowers sequentially. Never snap up or down. Instead, move smoothly. If discomfort occurs in your neck, lightly lace your fingers behind your head and neck for gentle support.

Crunches begin on your back with the knees flexed and feet flat on the floor. Cross your arms over your chest or lace the fingers lightly behind the back of the head. Exhale as you curl head, neck, and shoulders up sequentially. Draw the bottom of the rib cage

Crunches. Contract the abdominals and curl the upper back upward. Don't go too far or the feet will pop up off the floor.
Photo: Bruce Davis.

towards the top crest of the pelvis. Inhale as you lower to the starting position. Repeat these slowly so that you sense the sequential action. Then accelerate to a brisk pace. Repeat 8 times. Gradually increase to 50.

Pelvic Tilts begin on your back with knees flexed and feet flat on the floor. Contract the lower abdominals to tilt the coccyx and the back of the pelvis upward off the floor. Reverse, curling the pelvis downward to the original position. Keep your knees in line with the hips. Exhale as the pelvis lifts; inhale as the pelvis lowers. Do 8–32 tilts at a moderate tempo.

Vary this exercise by holding the knees together as the pelvis lifts. A second variation is to raise the pelvis as high as possible, almost arching the back. Like peeling a banana, sequentially lower the upper back, rib, waist, and pelvis to the floor.

The 100's begin on your back with knees flexed and feet flat on the floor. Curl the head and neck slightly off the floor; simultaneously lift and extend the feet slightly off the floor with extended knees. The hands are held in tight fists next to your hips. Briskly pulse the fists, vibrating them 100 times. The body remains in a dynamic space hold position, stretching away from the body center. Continue to breath naturally. Afterward, stretch the abdominals by reaching the arms overhead for at least 20 seconds. Once is enough for this one.

Bicycles are performed on your back, as though pedaling a bicycle. Draw the opposite elbow toward the knee when it flexes in to your chest. Maintain a vigorous pace, yet support the lower back by hollowing the lower abdominal area. Repeat 8–32 times.

Pelvic Tilts. Press the pelvis upward in a dynamic hinge position. Don't arch the back.
Photo: Bruce Davis.

The 100's. With feet and legs reaching long, pulse fists downward 100 times in holding and exhaling in sets of five pulses. Head and feet remain quiet.
Photo: Bruce Davis.

When doing bicycles, press the waist into the floor.
Photo: Bruce Davis.

Fan Kicks focus on the dynamic shifting in the body as it supports high kicks and leaps. Begin by laying on your back, arms pressing the floor next to the pelvis to stabilize the center of balance. Perform 4 small outward circles with a flexed gesture leg (*attitude*). Reverse, doing 4 small inward circles. Use 8 counts for each circle. The working leg crosses the body center slightly.

Once you isolate the action of the working thigh from a stabilized pelvis, repeat the exercise with a fully extended knee and foot. Avoid rolling the pelvis from side-to-side; keep the leg circle small enough to control.

Push-Ups

Push-Ups develop torso and arm strength enabling you to perform quick, ballistic isolations and falls or other transitions to the floor, like a jazz split. These movements must appear effortless. You must learn to synchronize the upper and lower areas of the body by increasing upper body strength to make finely tuned resilient motion possible.

Flexed Knee Push-Up begins in a prone position prone with knees flexed to a 90 degree angle, hands in line with the shoulders. Holding an extended torso, flex the elbows to lower the body toward the floor. Lifting the waist area, extend the elbows returning to the beginning position. If upper back and arms are weak, flex slightly at the hips to prevent low back strain. Repeat 5–30 times.

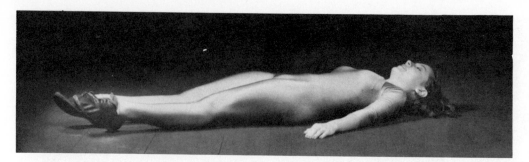

1. Begin fankicks by centering your body evenly with legs fully extended.
   Photo: Bruce Davis.

2. Draw leg across the center line without lifting the hip.
   Photo: Bruce Davis.

3. Complete the circle with a smile.
   Photo: Bruce Davis.

Repeat fankicks with straight legs.
Photo: Bruce Davis.

For safe push-up posture, flex slightly at the hips without arching the lower back.
Photo: Bruce Davis.

As your stretch increases, change to the fully extended push-up posture.
Photo: Bruce Davis.

Extended Knee Push-Up begins as above except to extend the knees, weight poised over the toes. The hips can be flexed slightly to reduce low back strain. If you have good arm and back strength, maintain a long, fully stretched body position. Flex the elbows, lowering to about 4 inches off the floor. Extend the elbows, returning to the beginning position. You must always retain correct form; repeat 1–2 times for women and 5–6 times for men. Progress to 20 repetitions for women and 50 for men.

Stride Stance Push-Up begins as before but with the legs in a comfortable side stance. Balance your weight evenly over the toes. Compress the waist area while performing a standard push-up. This is more advanced than the extended leg push-up, therefore do not attempt this exercise unless you're able to do at least 6 extended knee push-ups.

Mild Stretches

Use New Age or other harmonic music to encourage deep breathing and to release muscular tension during stretches. This enables relaxation and elasticity. Stretch in a slow, controlled manner. Allow a period of sustained holding when the fully stretched position is reached to gain maximum benefit. More intensive stretches may be done in the class to further develop muscle flexibility and the range of motion in the back, pelvis, and legs.

Sideward Lunge

Sideward Lunges emphasize the adductor (inner thigh) and gastrocnemius (calf) muscles. Stand in wide second position, arms in second. Grand plié slowly, keeping the torso erect. Curve the arms downward. Shift the pelvis over the right leg. (see Chapter Six for description of a lunge.) Place your hands on the floor in front of you to support the torso. Don't lift the right heel or drop the pelvis lower than knee level.

Gradually shift the pelvis back to center and recover the torso to vertical, arms opening to second. Inhale from the back of the waist as the knees extend and stretch the back of the knees. Alternate sides 4 times with each lunge.

Forward Lunge

Forward Lunges are performed fluidly to lengthen the quadriceps (front of the thigh) and the hip joint area. Stand in natural first position, arms curved downward.

Inhale slowly while stretching the right foot forward with the arms opening to a high V position. Exhale and soften the heel to shift forward onto a flexed right knee, foot flat on the floor. Lower to the floor in a deep lunge. Place your hands on the floor to support the weight of the torso. The back left foot is deeply flexed, toes curved under to support the leg. Fully stretch the left leg. Lift up the abdominals to reduce pelvic tilt and support the lower back.

Hold the position for 8 counts, breathing naturally. Recover by drawing the left foot into a natural first position. Extend both knees while the torso uncurls sequentially. Repeat by extending the right leg back.

Sideward lunge performed by Marcus Alford, artistic director Jazz Dance Theatre South.
Photo: Michael Canale.

This sideward lunge with left overcurve and a full horizontal reach is daring and dynamic without giving up technical accuracy.
Photo: TWU Dance Repertory Theatre.

Lunge deeply with forward leg at a right angle to stretch the hips and extend the thigh.
Photo: Bruce Davis.

Runner's Stretch

Runner's Stretch elongates the hamstrings, gastrocnemius, and achilles tendon as well as the gluteal muscles in the buttocks.

Continue from the forward lunge stretch of the previous exercise. Do not recover to a standing position. Instead, lift and shift the pelvis backward to extend both legs. Place your weight backward on to the right leg. With the torso inverted, slowly flex the forward left ankle while looking at the left knee.

Butterfly Press

Butterfly Press opens the hip joints and stretches the adductor muscles (inner thigh).

Seated in the butterfly position, clasp your ankles lifting the heels slightly to prevent over-stretching the outer edge of the ankle (called *sickling*). Hinge the torso forward while firmly pressing the knees open with the elbows. Hold for 8 counts, then recover to the beginning position. Repeat 4–8 times. For variety, cross the wrists and grasp the heels during the forward hinge.

Runner's stretch. Lift backward and upward while straightening the forward leg for a deep hamstring stretch.
Photo: Bruce Davis.

Butterfly Press. **Use the elbows to press the thighs open, stretching the adductor muscles of the inner thighs.**
Photo: Bruce Davis.

Second Position Stretches

Second Position Stretch maintains a sustained flow, changing smoothly from one position to the next to limber the waist and lower back, hip joints, and upper thigh. Anchor the pelvis to the floor and lift the abdominals strongly.

Begin seated, legs and arms extended to a front diagonal. Anchor the pelvis to the floor and strongly lift the abdominals. Lifting the torso out of the hips, turn to face the right leg and reach forward over the right thigh. In this position, circle the left arm forward, sideward, then upward to a high back diagonal. Focus on the path of the arm to look upward over the left shoulder. Lower to the right side stretch position. Circle the torso to the left, parallel to the floor; then raise to a vertical position, arms stretched sideward. Alternate directions 4 times.

Open Stance Stretch. Begin sitting in second position with the pelvis anchored and the ribs centered over the pelvis.
Photo: Bruce Davis.

Lifting out of the hips, turn to face the right leg. The back feels long.
Photo: Bruce Davis.

Sweep across the front space to reach strongly over the left leg.
Photo: Bruce Davis.

Lift to a vertical position while turning the spine and spiraling up to a high left focus.
Photo: Bruce Davis.

In the second part, reach to the right then circle continuously to the left side and recover to starting position.
Photo: Bruce Davis.

Hip Socket Creases

Hip Socket Creases increase your awareness of the natural pathway of the leg in forward extensions and how the leg and pelvis work together to stabilize movement of the gesture leg. Begin on your back, both legs stretched fully on the floor. The right knee bends deeply into the chest. Slowly extend it towards the ceiling. Lower the extended leg to the floor, flexing the foot. Drag the right heel into the floor as the right knee flexes to return to the beginning pose. Do not arch the back. Sense the support that the abdominals provide. Take 8 counts for each hip crease; do 6 creases with each leg. (This is called *développé*.)

Vary this exercise by reversing the path of the leg circle. For another variation, perform these two exercises in turn out. (Folding the leg towards the torso is called *enveloppé*.)

Back Pretzel

Back Pretzels stretch the deep gluteals and rotator muscles, controlling turn out.

Begin on your back, right knee bent with the foot flat on the floor. Hook the left ankle in front of the right knee. Lace your hands in back of the right leg. Lift the right foot off the floor and pull the right thigh towards the chest while pressing the left thigh open with the left elbow. Press the thigh open for 20 seconds, then relax. Repeat 4 times with each leg.

Hip socket creases utilize a smooth développé action with the leg and foot to warm up the hips.
Photo: Bruce Davis.

Designing Your Warm-Up

When organizing a warm-up routine, remember to move all the major zones of the body. Begin with slow and sustained movements then progress to brisk and vigorous actions.

Although it can be as brief as 8 minutes, target your routine at 15 minutes. Lengthen the routine if the temperature is cold to reach optimum muscular and mental readiness.

Are you working out on your own? Expand the routine to include more exercises to reach the desired workout time. Jazz, ballet, and modern techniques as described in the following chapters can be added. Jazz walks and connecting steps performed continuously for at least 20–30 minutes out of a total workout time of one hour increases the aerobic aspects of your workout. Monitor your heart rate to make sure you aren't overdoing it. Never work more than 70 percent of your maximum working heart rate.

One-pound wrist weights and wide rubber bands can be incorporated to add resistance and effort to arm and supported leg exercises. Avoid free swinging or highly ballistic arm or leg actions while using weights.

Use the following chart to note the exercises you have selected for your *Personal Warm-Up Routine.* Include at least one stretching and one strengthening exercise to ensure thorough conditioning of each major body zone. Refer to the anatomical figures in Chapter Three to check that you're working each area thoroughly.

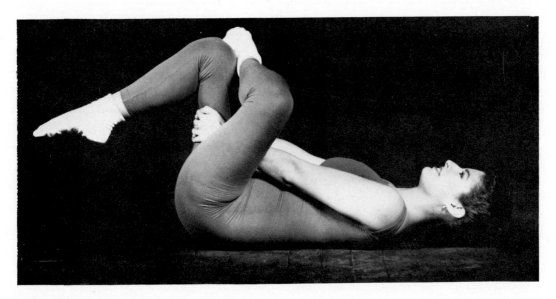

Pull the right thigh upward and open the left thigh in *pretzel* stretches.
Photo: Bruce Davis.

Personal Warm-up Chart

Category	Exercise Name	No. of Reps.	Page No.

Breathing

Arms and Torso

**Hip Joint and
Lumbar Spine**

**Abdominals and
Waistline**

Push-ups

Stretches

5

Principles of Dance Technique:

Applications for the Jazz Dancer

Up until now, we have described the essential components of a dance class as they are applied to jazz dancing. In this chapter, you will learn about ballet and modern techniques that have been adapted to jazz dancing. Keep in mind that there are many ways to stylize and interpret steps. We must first become familiar with the movements themselves and then see how they have been adapted to the jazz idiom, which we call *styling*. *Supporting leg* and *gesture leg* are two terms used throughout this chapter. Supporting leg refers to the leg that is balancing the body weight. The gesture leg is the leg that performs the movement or causes the action to occur. It bears no weight.

Ballet Theory and Fundamental Techniques

All theatrical dance forms have adopted the terminology, positions, and spatial directions codified in the eighteenth century French royal courts. Learning these terms is one of the initial steps you must take in order to communicate *how* and *where* to move. Borrowed from classical ballet, these formal ways of moving through space are the elements from which jazz poses, centered movements, and step patterns are constructed. Many jazz techniques have been adapted from classical ballet, especially turns and large movements like kicks and jumps. As you become familiar with individual ballet step patterns and poses, see how these classical movements are enlarged and distorted as they become building blocks for the jazz step patterns you will learn. Familiarize yourself with how the terms themselves relate to the actions that they represent.

One example is *plié,* a fundamental skill. It's more than a knee bend performed in a turned out position. It is a way of using the muscles of the leg. Integrating the leg to the pelvis and spine, a plié opens, widens, then lowers the body's center in a controlled, fluid manner. The same holds true for the positions of the feet and arms which involve the whole body. The torso is fully engaged with the act of supporting the arms, while the lower abdominals lift, supporting the pelvis and the hip. The inner thighs and buttocks muscles initiate turn-out in the legs.

Feet, Arm, and Basic Body Positions

Feet, Arm, and Basic Body Positions are pictured here. They are used by jazz dancers as well as by dancers of other western dance forms.

Pliés

Pliés develop elasticity in the leg muscles and strengthen the thigh, hip, and lumbar spine. The plié action controls the lowering and raising of the body during motion. Many steps begin and end in a plié for added spring, greater resiliency, and flow.

Demi plié refers to a half bend of the knees in which the body lowers until the heels almost begin to rise from the floor. Start in first position with a natural turnout. Actively press the inner thigh outward so that the knees flex and the center of weight begins to lower. Maintain a lifted alignment and do not permit the ankle and feet to roll in or out. A full stretch in the calves will be achieved when the heels can no longer remain on the floor. Extend the knees, pressing down into the floor through the forefoot, sensing a lift in the inner thighs.

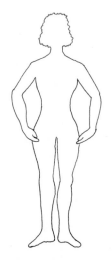

First Position.
Drawing by Craig Turski.

Second Position.
Drawing by Craig Turski.

Third Position.
Drawing by Craig Turski.

Fourth Position.
Drawing by Craig Turski.

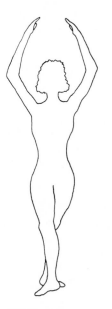

Fifth Position.
Drawing by Craig Turski.

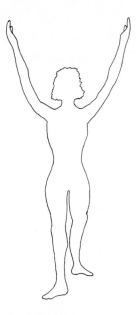

Sixth Position.
Drawing by Craig Turski.

Demi Plié (L) proper foot position (R) improper foot rolling in.
Photo: Bruce Davis.

Grand plié is a full bend in which the heels release (except in second position) and the body lowers until the thighs are almost parallel to the floor. Begin with a demi plié, then let the heels rise from the floor until the calves are fully stretched. The abdominals are strongly lifted. Good alignment throughout the plié action is imperative.

> Try this jazz sequence: Demi plié, in all five foot positions and grand plié in second and fourth only. Lower on counts one and two; raise to forced arches on counts three and four. Extend the knees fully (relevé) on counts five and six. Then lower the heels returning to the starting position on counts seven and eight. Now reverse the exercise. Relevé first, plié with forced arches, lower the heels to demi plié, then extend the knees to return to a standing position.

Relevé

Relevé is an action that raises the body up on to a three-fourth point position to balance on the balls (metatarsal joints) of the feet. Rising from floor level is another dimension of the dance vocabulary. Begin in first position with a natural turnout. Engage the inner thighs pressing them towards the body's center line and push down into the floor. The

Grand plié in second position.
Photo: Bruce Davis.

heels lift off the floor until you are supported only on the forefoot. Tighten the gluteals while keeping the torso and hips centered and the ankles aligned with the legs. Balance briefly, then slowly lower the heels, sensing the inner thighs pressing together.

> Try this jazz variation: Relevé strongly with bent knees. This is often called a *forced arch* foot position, one that is commonly used in lay-outs, turns, and balanced positions.

Battements

Battement is a term which describes several movements that use a beating action of the legs. The supporting leg is stationary while the gesture leg opens and then closes back to it. Battements are performed either parallel or turned out while brushing from any of the closed foot positions (1, 3, and 5). The gesture leg and foot extends, forcing the leg to escape to the open position. Following are four types of battements:

Battement Tendu is a gliding movement with a slight outward action. A sequential movement, battement tendu activates all parts of the foot (heel, arch, ball, and toe) to achieve a fully stretched leg and foot. The leg comes to a stop when the foot reaches a full extension with the tips of the toes in contact with the floor. The energy flow is then reversed (toe, ball, arch, and heel) to glide the foot back into the closed position.

> Try this jazz variation: Battement tendu to second position. Then plié on the supporting leg while placing weight on the gesture leg in the open position using a forced arch. Isolate a shoulder for added styling (see the end of this chapter for an in-depth description of isolation.)

Relevé in second position.
Photo: Bruce Davis.

Battement tendu in second position.
Photo: Bruce Davis.

Battement tendu in second position. CHI-TOWN Jazz Dance.
Photo by Ron Pomerantz.

Battement Dégagé is a small brushing action that stretches the foot and leg through the tendu position to a level slightly off the floor. This movement trains the foot and leg to disengage quickly as a preparation for jump sequences. It also shifts the weight onto one foot as a preparation for leg extensions or kicks. Therefore it is essential that the movement be small and close to the floor. The outward thrust of energy in the leg propels the foot to escape slightly off the floor (only a few inches). The movement stops momentarily before the reverse closing action occurs.

Try this jazz variation: Perform a series of battement dégagé while in demi plié. Keep the gesture foot in a forced arch position only brushing with the ball of the foot. The pelvis remains still throughout the movement.

Grand Battement is a large beat, a controlled movement in which the gesture leg performs a high kick. A downward thrust motivates the leg to escape into a genuine kick to peak usually hip level or higher. Then the energy must be gathered back in as the leg is lowered in a controlled manner. The force of the kick is countered by a strong oppositional lift in the supporting hip and a conscious shift of the center over the supporting leg.

Try this jazz variation: Perform a series of swing kicks using a box step pattern. Begin in demi plié, parallel first position and with each subsequent step, maintain demi plié level. Step right straight back on count one, then step left directly to the side on count two, step right forward on count three, execute a large swing kick to the front on count four. Repeat the pattern to the other side.

Battement dégagé in second position.
Photo: Bruce Davis.

Grand battement in jazz relevé.
Photo: Bruce Davis.

Sur le cou de pied position.
Photo: Jennifer Collins.

Rond de jambe—forward position.
Photo: Bruce Davis.

Rond de jambe—second position.
Photo: Bruce Davis.

Rond de jambe—back position.
Photo: Bruce Davis.

Battement Frappé is a striking movement of the gesture leg against the floor. Begin with your weight shifted onto the left. Lift the right foot and hold it at the left ankle with an extended foot. This foot gesture position is called *sur le cou de pied* (at the neck of the foot). From this starting position, brush the right foot down and out to dégagé in second position striking the floor with a forceful action ending fully extended a few inches above the floor. The movement stops momentarily, and then the foot quickly returns to *sur le cou de pied* position. Keep the gesture knee stable; don't allow any twisting to occur. Frappés are usually performed in a series to the front, side, and back.

Try this jazz variation: Start with the working foot in a forced arch touching the floor at the base of the supporting leg. Now perform a series of flicking kicks thrusting the leg to the extended position with a snappy kick action.

Rond de Jambe

Rond de Jambe is a circling motion involving the entire gesture leg. The pelvis adjusts dynamically to support this large action. The foot literally draws a half circle on the floor. Begin in a turned out first position. Tendu the right foot forward. With the tip of the toe, circle the leg to second; continue to the back until the toe reaches tendu position; now close the foot through first position. Maintain your turnout throughout the entire circle; avoid tilting the pelvis. The movement can also be reversed by beginning to the back. *Remember this important concept* which is illustrated again in fan kicks and piqué and pirouette turns: when circling from front to back, the movement will create an outward motion (*en dehors,* to the outside); when circling from the back to the front, your movement is inward (*en dedans,* to the inside).

Try this jazz variation: Perform the rond de jambe with a leading hip isolation, imitating the movement with the pelvis. Contract (see modern fundamentals) during each hip thrust forward or back to emphasize count one of the movement.

Modern Theory and Fundamental Techniques

The twentieth century ushered in a revolution in how dancers viewed their world. Instead of relying on traditional forms of expression, like classical ballet, they decided first why and what they wanted to dance and then how. Form followed function. Modern dancers began a more individualized and psychologically expressive approach toward choreography. Jazz dancers borrowed a number of these theories of movement to enlarge their creative range. Dancers, from Katherine Dunham and Fred Astaire to Paula Abdul and Bob Fosse, have improvised personally distinctive motifs applying different theories as a basis for their choreography. Studying these concepts will allow you to begin experiencing the various approaches which shape new directions in contemporary jazz choreography.

Contraction

Contraction is a controlled withdrawal or retreat of the torso from the body's center line. For modern dancers, the contraction often symbolizes the inner yearning of the soul making the movement and gesture more personally expressive. To perform a contraction, begin by standing in a neutral position, heels together with your weight properly centered. Sense your center, and focus mentally on the area directly below the rib cage and above the hip girdle. Slowly pull back through your center, actively lifting the abdominals up under the rib cage. Breath out fully thereby deepening or hollowing the spine into a concave curve. Don't collapse; maintain a stable shoulder girdle and lifted chest as the hips tilt upward slightly. Contractions may also be done quickly, in a sudden motion. Imagine retreating as if you were being punched in the stomach.

> Try this jazz variation: Contraction in demi plié first position. Add a double shoulder isolation by hunching sharply forward. Now walk deliberately forward snapping your fingers with each step. (See the beatnik walk in Chapter Six).

Fall and Recovery

Fall and Recovery is a dynamic way to use space more fully. The floor or the area below the body's center is used as freely as the space above. Always a powerful force, the effect of gravity is visualized when a dancer suddenly changes levels through controlled

Contraction with a parallel passé in jazz relevé.
San Francisco Jazz Dance Co.

falling. Sensing the outward centrifugal force in conjunction with gravity will help you discover many ways to master low-level changes.

Variations of falling occur in all directions, front, side, and back. Front falls quite often use a tilting action, while side and back falls tend to collapse through the body's center. A side fall, for example, starts with a swinging motion, incorporating a natural falling action to build momentum. To perform a side fall, start on your knees with your arms overhead. Swing the arms simultaneously to the left; crossing in front of the body, lower to sit on the heels. Continue sweeping the arms to the right and slide your body out on the floor until you are fully extended and lying on your right side. Recover by rolling onto your back then curl up to a sitting position.

Try this jazz variation: Begin in a turned out third position. Slowly execute a forward split. As you slide forward to a wide fourth position catch the floor with your outside hand. Continue your descent to the floor bending the back knee to an attitude position (see balanced techniques). Use your arm for added support. Recover by swinging the back leg around and stepping through to a standing position. This is called a *jazz split*.

Side fall from the knees.
Photo: Bruce Davis.

Sliding into a jazz split.
Photo: Bruce Davis.

Using the breath correctly helps propel the dancer into the air. Lynn Dally and Sam Weber.
Photo: Judy Francesconi.

Breath

Breath is a controlled use of air that emphasizes your natural body rhythm. It gets you more in tune with yourself while helping you to discover the proper amount of energy needed for a particular step. Incorporating a conscious use of breath, the dancer is able to initiate and manipulate different conditions of muscular tension. For example, a state of total ease versus great anxiety can be visualized and expressed through the use of breath. Remember Michael Jackson's *Thriller?* Breath effectively emphasized the pulsing weighted steps of the panting creatures as they emerged from their slumbering underworld domain. Breath can also increase the feel and look of lightness by lifting the torso.

Spirals

Spirals are movements that twist or corkscrew the body. Since the torso usually moves in opposition to the lower body, the resulting movement has a disconnected look due to three-dimensional shaping. Combining a spiral with a deep plié is an effective transition to the floor and from the floor to a standing level.

Try this jazz variation: Stand in a parallel second position. Leaving the feet firmly planted, execute a half turn of the upper body, facing to the back. For more torque, add a demi plié while executing the half turn.

A spiral position.
Jazz Master Gus Giordano.

Using natural gesture.
Photo: Bruce Davis.

Natural Gesture

Natural Gesture is often enlarged as an overly emphasized posture. It is your bodily attitude responding to a situation. Sometimes your reaction can be a natural impulse or a culturally learned derivative. For example in Michael Jackson's *Moonwalk,* his now familiar walk was a caricature, an eye-catching exaggeration! For a dancer, natural gesture is a starting point to understanding a situation that might have occurred in life. The dancer creatively alters the gestural attitude to express the image without necessarily making a clearly defined statement. For example, a dancer might communicate confusion by grasping both sides of the head with the hands and then slashing the arms from side to side in abrupt sweeping motions.

> Try this jazz variation: Stare at an object and let the angle of your look distort your posture. Take 8 counts to assume the pose. Hold it for 4 counts, make it even bigger for 2 counts, then quickly recover in 2 counts.

Abstraction

Abstraction occurs when the dancer initiates movement with a gesture and then enlarges, distorts, or enhances the image through a manipulation of the elements of space, time, and/or energy. Contemporary dancers have not been content to show psychological stress like heartbreak, for example, by beating the chest with the fists as has been done in early ballets. Codified ways of expressing emotion were limiting. They saw them as

Using Abstract Gesture Dance Stop Company in "Silly Samba" by Annie Day.
Photo: Denny Cohen.

superficial expressions of deeply felt emotion. Both the variety and universality of the human spirit were expressed through their unique interpretations. Today, gesture is a jumping off point for the dancer who uses various ways to expand, personalize, and exaggerate movement.

Centered Jazz Techniques

Movements that occur around the body's natural center of gravity do not travel, so they are especially suited to coordinating arm and leg actions. Centered movements are stationary poses involving various arm and leg gestures, movements that twist and bend the torso. They have the potential for a wide range of dynamic and expressive energy and are integral to creative jazz choreography.

Isolations

Isolations are brief, small movements that highlight one area of the body at a time. Adopted from East Indian *mudras,* they are used to warm up, build strength, release tension in the joints, and add color, focus, syncopation, and variety to a movement sequence. Almost any body part that can move independently can be isolated. Individual range of motion and natural joint movement preferences will vary, but isolations can and should be executed without discomfort or pain in the joints. Abdominal support and good alignment are required for isolations. Isolations may be practiced singly much as a pianist practices scales, but dancers use isolations as part of the overall design of a dance phrase.

Work to synchronize movements to essential rhythmic structures of music. An isolation exercise is varied by changing rhythm, tempo, spatial range of action or dynamics. Manipulation of any one of these factors will alter the kinetic movement quality.

Following are examples of how to play with these factors:

1. *Sustained and steady flow* produces rotational and rhythmically even movements.
2. *Accented flow* emphasizes parts of a beat in a rhythmic pattern.
3. *Syncopated flow* switches the accents to the off-beat counts giving a feeling of spontaneity and anticipation.

Isolations are used within thematic dance material to vary the rhythmic as well as stylistic options or choices. Their design is related directly to the movement potential of the joint area itself and includes the head and neck, shoulders, rib cage, and hip girdle. Sustained, accented, or syncopated rhythms add even greater variety to your isolations. For example, move the shoulders in a smooth sustained circle. Accent the top of the circle or at other points within the circle to add syncopation. Following are more examples of how these body parts can be isolated.

Head and Neck Starting from a neutral position, press the shoulders down, (with the chin in and the ears over the shoulders.)

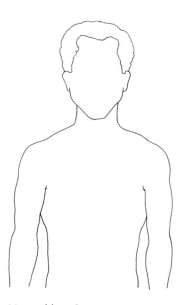

Neutral head position.
Drawing by Craig Turski.

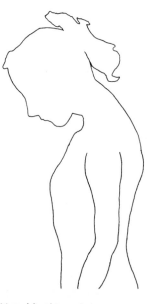

Head looking down.
Drawing by Craig Turski.

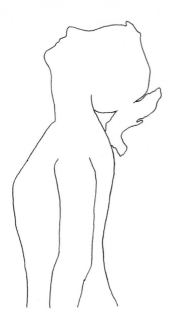

Head looking up.
Drawing by Craig Turski.

Head moving right to left.
Drawing by Craig Turski.

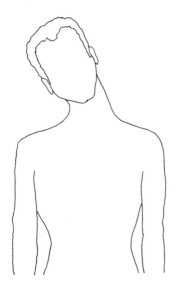

Head dropped to the right side.
Drawing by Craig Turski.

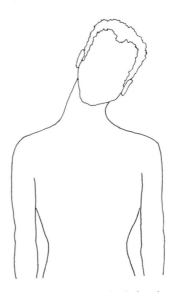

Head dropped to the left side.
Drawing by Craig Turski.

Head dropping side-to-side (ear to shoulder).
Photo: Bruce Davis.

The head rotating in a circle.
Photo: Bruce Davis.

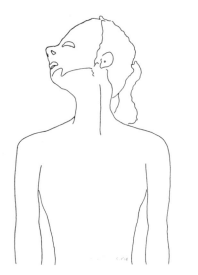

Head rotating to the right in a backward circle.
Drawing by Craig Turski.

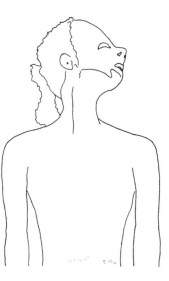

Head rotating to the left in a backward circle.
Drawing by Craig Turski.

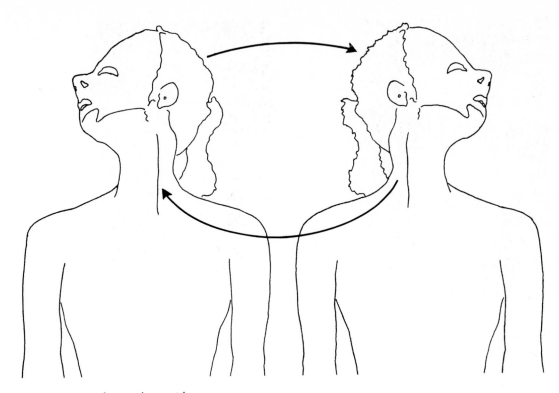

Head swinging from side-to-side.
Drawing by Craig Turski.

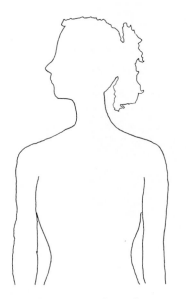

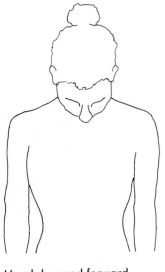

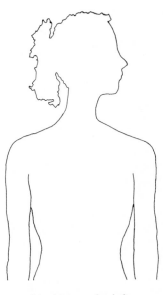

Head dropped forward.
Drawing by Craig Turski.

Head looking to the right.
Drawing by Craig Turski.

Head looking to the left.
Drawing by Craig Turski.

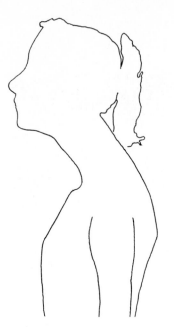

Head shifted forward.
Drawing by Craig Turski.

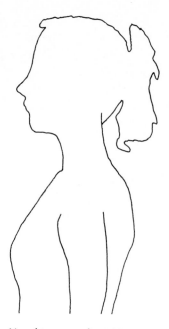

Head in neutral position.
Drawing by Craig Turski.

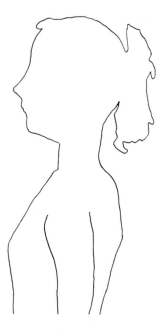

Head shifted backward.
Drawing by Craig Turski.

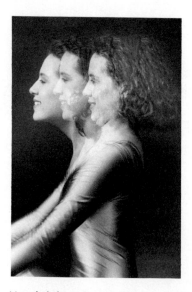

Head shifting forward and back from neutral position.
Photo: Bruce Davis.

Shoulder isolations can be performed together or independently, in simultaneous directions, or in opposition.

Shoulder isolation; shrugging up and down.
Al Germani Dance Co. in "Tux."

Shoulder pressed forward in the dig position.
Photo: Bruce Davis.

Shoulder circle—forward.
Photo: Bruce Davis.

Shoulder circle—lifted.
Photo: Bruce Davis.

Shoulder circle—to the back.
Photo: Bruce Davis.

Shoulder rotating forward.
Photo: Bruce Davis.

Rib Cage isolations exaggerate the separation between the ribs and pelvis, always lifting the ribs with the abdominals.

Rib cage isolations; shifting forward.
Photo: Bruce Davis.

Shifting back.
Photo: Bruce Davis.

Shifting to the side.
Photo: Bruce Davis.

Circling to the right.
Photo: Bruce Davis.

Circling to the left.
Photo: Bruce Davis.

Hip Girdle isolations are performed with the knees released in a demi plié position in order to achieve maximum range of motion without straining the lumbar spine.

Tilting the hip girdle side-to-side.
Photo: Jennifer Collins.

Hip girdle circle and swing.
Photo: Bruce Davis.

Experiment with these different kinds of isolation movements. Practice them independently first using a variety of rhythmic patterns. Increase the challenge by combining isolation movements of different body parts. Start out by designing a basic arm pattern in a four-count phrase such as: arms out to the side on count one, fold arms into the chest from the elbow on count two, back to the side on count three, arms down to the side on count four.

Now, add a four-count isolation sequence of the head, shoulders, rib cage, or hips. First move laterally from side to side. Once this has been mastered, try varying the rhythm, tempo, or beat. Following are some common jazz variations:

1. Combine two different isolation movements concurrently or sequentially, such as moving the hips smoothly and the arms percussively.
2. Add a walk pattern, as described in Chapter Six.
3. Mirror the quality, the dynamics, and/or the tempo of different types of music.
4. Syncopate the rhythmic pattern so that the movement is not in straight counts. For example, move on counts one and two, hold count three and move again on count four. Or hold on count one, move on counts two, three, and four.

Southwest Jazz Ballet hip isolations from "Top Gun-Danger Zone."
Photo: Jay Storr.

5. Try *snaking*; a sequential thrusting of the head, neck, shoulders, rib, and hip girdle to the same direction, accompanied by a lean into that foot. The movement alternates sides or can be done front to back.
6. Try a *shimmy*; a vibratory shaking action isolating the upper torso initiated by the shoulders.
7. Try the *twist*; a rotating action of the pelvis and torso.

As you can see, the possibilities are unlimited and depend only on your imagination, creativity, and determination to invent and perfect a uniquely stylish pattern.

Passé

Passé is a leg gesture which can be performed turned out, parallel, or even turned in across the body's center line. Begin in a natural first position. Transfer the weight on to the left foot by slightly shifting the body's center. Now draw the right foot up the side of the left leg with the foot fully extended. Keep lifting until the tip of the toe touches the

Parallel passé in relevé.
Photo: Bruce Davis.

Forward lunge.
Photo: Bruce Davis.

inside of the left knee. If beginning in third or fifth position, the foot moves on a diagonal line across the supporting leg, finishing with the toe to the side of the knee. A passé can be held for a balance or a turn before it returns to the starting closed position.

> Try this jazz variation: Perform a passé in parallel position. Lift the arms to sixth position while lifting the working hip in an isolation. Add a relevé and a chest release when you feel comfortable with the balance on a flat foot. This powerful position can add a truly dynamic moment in any jazz choreography.

Lunge

Lunge is a versatile and vigorous looking standing position that is used in combination with various movements. It is a wide base of support, or an exaggerated open position in either second or fourth. In a lunge, only one leg is bent. That leg is considered the supporting leg even though the center weight is not directly over it. Because of the wide stance, the weight is centered slightly behind the supporting leg. The second leg is fully extended in the open position and rests on a flat foot. Arm, head, shoulder, rib cage, and even some limited hip isolations can be performed in a lunge. It is also used for various stretch exercises and as a preparation for inside turns.

Hinge action. Jazzdance: The Danny Buraczeski Dance Co. "Fission" with April Hinkle and Jim Viera.
Photo: Jack Mitchell.

Hinges and Tilts

Hinges and Tilts are movements that shift, lean, or incline dramatically. The hinge or tilt begins at the knees or hips. The upper body is usually held firmly in a diagonal line (oblique) from the point of the hinged joint. Tilts are performed to the front, back, or side. The entire length of the torso can be involved from head to hips, or the hinged tilt can be made at the waist, focusing only on the upper body. Shape the arms in a way to help maintain balance.

Try these jazz variations:

1. Begin in turned out second position in a demi plié. Deepen the plié on the right leg shifting into it while stretching the left leg to a fully extended tendu. Simultaneously tilt the body to a high right diagonal until you achieve a straight line from the left toe to the tip of the head. To increase the oblique line, stretch the left arm over the head following the line.

Side lunge.
Photo: Bruce Davis.

Back lunge.
Photo: Bruce Davis.

2. Begin on your knees. Lunge forward by tilting from the hip joint while keeping the upper torso rigid. Hinge backward by deepening the flexion of the knee. The abdominals must be held firmly so that strain is not put on the lumbar back muscles. Only tilt as far as you can control the torso and maintain a straight line without undue stress on the thigh and back muscles.

For other jazz variations, see the Cakewalk and Trenches in Chapter Six.

Balanced Jazz Techniques

Dance movements often necessitate balancing on one foot. Balanced body positions are usually spectacular movements that fully integrate your strength, flexibility, timing, and balance. Remember that all balances rely on the primary principle of centering the body's weight over the supporting leg. Centering must be carried through onto the ball of the foot as the dancer rises in a relevé. The supporting hip is aligned over the foot. All pliés should be executed carefully to prevent inward rotating of the knees.

The arms are used to form a balanced spatial design of balanced positions. They move through formal positions, but should always be energized to counterbalance the lifted leg and help reverse the energy field created by the supporting leg. (Refer to the principle of opposition and other principles of movement that are applied in all balanced body positions in Chapter Three).

Arabesque

Arabesque, the most common of the balanced body positions, is a simple, elegant back leg extension. Leg extensions are also done to the front or to the side. A slight adjustment of the center of weight into the supporting hip along with a controlled tilting of the pelvis is required to achieve an arabesque. These adjustments compensate for the added weight of the leg as it extends backward. Never drop your weight into the supporting hip joint and "sit on" the leg. Greater height of the extended leg can be achieved if turnout is used. This frees the natural resistance in the hip socket and allows a fuller range of motion in the joint. Both the rib cage and pelvis tilt forward to achieve an arabesque above a 45 degree angle. Hold the back strongly during the forward adjustment while the abdominal muscles remain taut throughout. The higher the elevation of the gesture leg, the greater the displacement of the rib cage and pelvis. Remember to keep the rib cage lifted away from the hip girdle as the entire spine extends.

Attitude

Attitude is a balanced body position in which the gesture leg is bent in a 45 to 90 degree angle. Involving the same principles as an arabesque, an attitude can be performed to the front, side, or back. The height of the extended knee may vary, but turnout is essential to create the proper shaping of the position inspired by a classic statue of the Greek god Mercury.

Lay-Outs

Lay-Outs are balanced jazz body poses involving a dramatically tilted torso. Peformed in a demi plié or jazz relevé, lay-outs are more difficult to control than straight leg support balances because the knee joint is not extended and therefore is susceptible to rotation injuries. Although the dancer appears to be precariously poised, the principle of oppositional force is again applied to achieve a stable balance. Although there may be several lay-out variations, following are three simple versions.

Second Arabesque with downward focus. TWU Dance Repertory Theater.
Photo: Jennifer Collins.

Back attitude.
Photo: Bruce Davis.

Side attitude.
Photo: Bruce Davis.

Front lay-out. Jazzdance: The Danny Buraczeski Dance Co. in "Avalon" with Robert Smith and Jane Blont.
Photo: Jack Mitchell.

In *front* lay-outs, the dancer executes a back leg extension as the upper body hinges forward to a point parallel to the floor. A slow progressive demi plié accompanies the back leg extension which counterbalances the forward pitched position of the upper body. Both supporting and gesture legs may be turned out or parallel. Extend your arms either overhead or to second position aiding the balance.

In *side* lay-outs the hip joint of the supporting leg acts as the hinge point of the balance. This lay-out is usually executed in a parallel or a modified turn-out. As the leg is lifted, the upper body tilts to the opposite side. The front of the body faces forward while the arms extend overhead on a line relative to the body. A slight demi plié occurs as the extension progresses.

Back lay-outs are the most difficult of the three lay-outs. This position requires a forward leg extension and a high back release. Strong abdominal muscles are essential to prevent a break in the lumbar and/or thoracic areas of the back possibly straining the spine. Only the head, upper back, and rib cage extend backward to counterbalance the forward extended leg. The head and neck remain aligned with the angle of the upper body extension. Press the upper chest towards the ceiling by lifting the rib cage separating it from the abdominals. Focus on a point where the wall and ceiling meet to prevent breaking the line of the upper spine. Never strain the neck by dropping the head back. Again, execute a slight demi plié slowly with the extensions.

Side lay-out with a lift.

Back lay-out.
Photo: Bruce Davis.

6

Adding a Little Spice:
Moving Through Space

Dance is concerned with making a statement and communicating an idea through movement. In order to accomplish this goal, dancers learn to move both expressively and efficiently. In the last chapter we explored a whole realm of movement that occurs around the body's center while it remains relatively fixed in space. Mastering these techniques builds strength, agility, flexibility, range, and confidence within your movement potential.

Now imagine sitting in your bedroom all day, never leaving that limited area! After awhile the beckoning urge to explore beyond the familiar surroundings of that room overwhelms you. So too, you will want to strike out and discover a larger range of jazz movements; ones that propel the body through and around the dance studio. The question now becomes not merely how do I shape the body, but how is that shape carried through space? How is the image of energy expressed?

The art of dance occurs *between* the positions, not *at* the positions. The ballet dancer gives the illusion of overcoming gravity by appearing to move effortlessly, gently flowing through the space, while maintaining strict posturing. The modern dancer penetrates the space by creating an environment that works in partnership with the floor, making use of inherent movement tendencies. These natural movements include falling and recovering, torso contractions, extensions, spirals, hinges and tilts, and multiple body focuses.

The jazz dancer creates a movement statement in many varied ways: by skimming the floor with bursts of energy; by controlling dramatically deliberate movements; by whipping the space with powerful torso actions; and by escaping gravity with spectacular jumps, kicks, and turns. Jazz dance is unique because it so closely relates to the social conditions of human life, emphasizing both physical and emotional expressiveness. Reflecting the needs, dreams, outrage, desires, and emotions of the times, jazz dancers can quiver with delight, reel with sorrowful mourning, shake with jubilation, collapse from a tension-filled moment, sway in celebration, or punch out a powerful message. Think about the depression era of the 1930s. The extravagant musical became a popular form of escape from a sometimes downtrodden existence. In the late 1950s, Alvin Ailey's *Revelations* was an exciting representation of the conditions and individuality of the black American culture. In both cases, jazz dance expressed intimate and very personal movement experiences inspired by the times.

The dancer's task is to synthesize rhythmic impulses and proper dance technique through outbursts of creative energy. This synthesis is demonstrated as a free flowing expression of the inner self. Interject your personality while dancing so that you are supporting new challenges with an open and positive attitude. Mistakes are a natural part of experiencing and growing. Success will come with practice. Therefore, allow yourself to enjoy the sensation of movement as you walk, run, skip, slide, and explore the space *jazz style*.

Southwest Jazz Ballet Co. in "All That Jazz."
Photo: Jay Storr.

Walks

Walking is a natural building block in the jazz choreographer's repertoire. Simply stated, walking is the shifting of weight from one foot to the other while moving the body through space. But the variety of ways to accomplish these weight shifts is practically endless.

The dance walk transports the center of gravity through space in a smooth and efficient manner. Usually a slight plié position is assumed. Your weight rides on the balls of the feet so that as the weight transfers to the new foot, the second leg propels the body in the intended direction.

The basic dance walk is transformed by refining it to fit a theme or image that is being created. You design or stylize the dance walk by adding to or changing the various detailed parts that make up the movement. How is this accomplished? Alter the spatial direction of the walk, vary the tempo, alternate the dynamic impact, or shift the body level. Isolation movements may be added as described in Chapter Five. Following are some basic walk patterns for you to practice.

Jazz Walk

Jazz Walk is catlike yet assertive in its control of the space. Begin in first position demi plié. Step forward on the right leg, lightly rolling through the foot, beginning with the toe, until the heel barely touches the floor. The left leg thrusts the body forward to lengthen the stride during the weight transfer. Finish the step in demi plié then repeat to the left. Swing the arms naturally to an open third position in opposition to each step. Here are some more variations.

1. Press the shoulders in opposition with each step.
2. Pendulum swing the arms from the elbows adding a finger snap with each step.
3. Isolate a hip with each step; thrust the leading hip diagonally forward. The right hip leads to a forward diagonal with the right step and the left when stepping on the left.

Relevé Walk

Relevé Walk stays in a continuous high level in an abrupt, almost fussy manner. Begin in first position relevé with a slight turnout. Staying in relevé, step on the right foot directly in front of the left. Repeat with the left as if walking on a tight rope.
Other variations include:

1. Increase the crossover beyond the center body line to a slight diagonal front step, sometimes called a *sugar* or *French twist*.
2. Place the arms in a high V position and isolate the shoulders in opposition, up and then back in place with each step.

Basic jazz walk.
Photo: Bruce Davis.

Relevé walk.
Photo: Bruce Davis.

Beatnik Walk

Beatnik Walk is a low-level walk which gives a sneaky, cool, down-low look. Begin in first position with the elbows tight to the body, forearms forward and wrists turned upward. Hunch forward and assume the deepest demi plié possible, then rush forward snapping your fingers on each step.

Strut

Strut is a variation of the jazz walk that utilizes a high chest release, much like a drum major leading the band. Begin as a jazz walk but lift the chest proudly and project to forward high. Increase the length of the stride and thrust the body through the space leading with the chest.

Dig

Dig is a common movement in jazz that rhythmically delays a weight transfer. A dig is most often used for emphasis, rhythmic accent, or to add dynamics to the movement phrase. A dig occurs when you vigorously tap the ball of the free foot on the floor without transferring weight. The dig is usually performed in a closed foot position on an *and* count, but can also be done in an open position, especially when coming out of an attitude or series of turns. Since the dig foot is not weight bearing, the next step will occur on that foot.

Beatnik walk.
Photo: Bruce Davis.

Strut.
Photo: Bruce Davis.

Step Dig

Step Dig is executed in any direction: front, side, back, or to the diagonal. Remain in demi plié position. Begin in first position with parallel feet. Step forward with the right and close, tapping (digging) the ball of the left foot to the right. Be sure to accent the dig abruptly with the music. Repeat to the left.

Try this variation: Execute the step dig to the side in a slight diagonal direction, alternating feet.

Attitude Walk

Attitude Walk is a smooth forward progressive movement with no visible level change. Step forward on the right, carefully rolling down through the foot. As the left leg pushes the body forward onto the right, raise the left leg to a low back attitude. Engage the abdominals and extend the gesture foot. The arms swing naturally from the elbows with each step, and the body appears to slink through the space. Repeat on the left.

Step dig (the step).
Photo: Bruce Davis.

Step dig (the dig).
Photo: Bruce Davis.

Attitude walk.
Photo: Bruce Davis.

Hillbilly walk.
Photo: Bruce Davis.

Hillbilly Walk

Hillbilly Walk gives you a feeling of a country western hoedown. Step forward with a straight leg onto the heel instead of on the ball of the foot. Add a bouncy demi plié with each weight transfer and a hand clap on the offbeats.

Calypso Walk

Calypso Walk is a Latin-American walk that moves to the side. Begin in parallel first, demi plié and face the left diagonal. Step with straight legs to the side onto the left foot. Thrust or pop the right hip to right side high allowing the right heel to come off the floor as the weight transfer is completed. Dig the right foot to the left staying on the ball of the foot, resuming a plié position sharply accenting the right hip to the high right side. Always accent the outward step of the walk. Continue to the right, pushing off the right foot that is still in a dig position. Change to a right direction by shifting the weight onto the right and then digging the right. Arms swing front and back with each step, or add shoulder isolations that lift, circle, or shimmy. A *rumba* combines a forward calypso walk and two steps in a slow-quick-quick rhythm.

Cakewalk

Cakewalk is a dance step that originated during sporting contests on plantations (refer to Chapter Nine) in which a cake was awarded to the winner. It is a strut with a leg lift added to each step. Strut forward onto the right and swing the left leg forward to front attitude. Repeat on the other leg. Keep progressing forward, adding a bounce or hop to each step. The arms remain in a stationary position such as crossed in front of the lifted chest, held down at the sides, or vibrating in an open hand position.

Connecting Steps

Connecting steps link larger steps to create movement phrases. Their purpose is to build momentum within a locomotor pattern; they are usually not emphasized. They can, however, demonstrate a wide range of dynamic impulses and create rhythmic variations, or changes in the flow, level, emphasis and direction of the dance phrase. Think of them as transitions in space and time that bond steps together as a holistic jazz dance.

Calypso walk.
Photo: Bruce Davis.

Cakewalk (the strut step).
Photo: Bruce Davis.

Cakewalk (the lift).
Photo: Bruce Davis.

Grapevine (step to the side).
Photo: Bruce Davis.

Grapevine (crossing in back).
Photo: Bruce Davis.

Grapevine (crossing in front).
Photo: Bruce Davis.

Grapevine

Grapevine is a traveling step found in many traditional folk dances. It is named for the weaving pattern created by the feet resembling grapevine branches. The step usually moves side-to-side either to the right or to the left. Step sideward on to the right foot. Continue progressing to the right by crossing the left in back of the right across the body's centerline. Repeat the right side step and then cross the left in front. Continue alternating the cross step back and front between each side step. Be sure to remain in demi plié. For styling, rise to relevé with each side step, or pulse one hip or shoulder.

Two-Step

Two-Step is also a traditional folk step and is common to many social dances. The two-step is a step-close-step pattern that alternates sides. This traveling step is executed to any direction and in various floor patterns and rhythms. Step out on the right to the side. Bring the left into a closed position, then take another step out on the right. The step is easily repeated alternating sides and is commonly done traveling forward and backward.

Pas de Bourrée

Pas de Bourrée is a basic ballet transition movement consisting of three small steps. Take a small step with the left foot behind the right, crossing the body's centerline. Progress to the right side by taking a small right side step. Complete the three-step pattern with a left step on the center line of the body in front of the supporting leg. Reverse the pattern. The three steps are performed in two counts; step *one*, step *and*, step *two*. Pas de bourrée may be executed by crossing under (*dessous*) or over (*dessus*) the

Two-Step (step close step).
Photo: Bruce Davis.

Pas de bourreé (left foot steps behind).
Photo: Bruce Davis.

Pas de bourreé (the side step).
Photo: Bruce Davis.

Pas de bourreé (left foot steps in front).
Photo: Bruce Davis.

supporting leg. Other variations include stepping side-side-back or back-side-side. Although it is usually executed in relevé, pas de bourrée is also often done in jazz relevé or in demi plié.

Cross Step

Cross Step crosses over the body's center line while traveling through space. The step alternates sides to progress forward or backward. There are many variations, but here are three of the most popular forms.

Cross touch begins in first position. Step with the left across the body's center line. Then dig the ball of the right foot to second position. Without transferring the weight onto the right foot, continue the movement forward by repeating the cross step on the

Cross touch (the cross step).
Photo: Bruce Davis.

Cross touch (the touch).
Photo: Bruce Davis.

Cross kick (the cross step).
Photo: Bruce Davis.

Cross kick (the kick).
Photo: Bruce Davis.

115

right digging the left foot to second. Move backward with a cross step behind the supporting leg. Vary this step by remaining in demi plié or rising to a relevé on the cross step. Add head or shoulder isolations with each dig, or perhaps a hip thrust to stylize!

Cross Kick is executed the same as cross touch but instead of digging the free foot in second, loosely kick the foot to second, to the front, or to the back. Extend the gesture leg and foot fully with each kick without snapping the knee. Continue by repeating it to the other side. Cross step on the left, kick the right, then cross step on the right and kick the left. For styling, add head, shoulder, or arm isolations with each step.

Cross Ball Change begins as before but this time a small weight transfer will occur on the second leg as you execute a ball change, usually in second or fourth position. A ball change is a rocking step, a small, quick weight transfer onto the ball of the foot and then back to the other foot. It only uses an *and* count. Cross step right over the left foot. Transfer the weight onto the ball of the right foot momentarily while it is reaching out to the second position. Recover onto the right, maintaining a second position. Repeat the movement to the left beginning with right cross step. Always cross step to a forward or back diagonal if you are traveling in a forward or backward direction.

Now add arm, head, shoulder, rib, or hip isolations. Start out with a simple pattern and then layer a new isolation movement with each eight-count phrase.

Cross ball change.
Photo: Bruce Davis.

Chassé

Chassé is a French term meaning "to chase." Chassé can be executed in any direction and is considered an aerial movement because both feet leave the ground. In jazz, however, it may also be executed while maintaining plié. Chassé is a series of progressing steps that form a step-close pattern. The leading leg is chased by the second, then a small quick weight transfer occurs as the leading leg takes another step. Reach forward on the right foot. Bring the left leg into fifth position as you transfer the weight lightly onto the left foot. The left leg literally replaces the right directly underneath your center. Then step forward again onto the right.

Repeat in a series. Once you are comfortable with the weight transfer, put more energy into each step. Increase the speed of the weight change so that you are lifted into the air. Fully extend both legs in a tight fifth position, toes pointed, as you transfer from right to left. The speed and energy of the chassé creates a momentum that will propel you in the line of direction. Thrusting hip isolations that initiate the step create exciting movement impulses. Variations include:

1. Chassé sideways, backwards, or in a circular pattern.
2. A turning chassé is a brilliant transition. So experiment with a complete or half turn in the air (*saut de basque*). As with any turn, spot your landing (see Chapter Seven for spotting and turns).

Chassé.
Photo: Bruce Davis.

Jazz square (step 1—front cross step).
Drawing by Craig Turski.

Jazz square (step 2—step backward).
Drawing by Craig Turski.

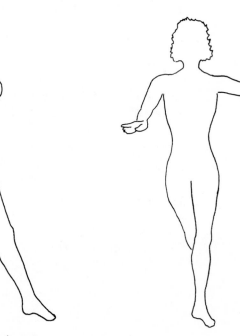

Jazz square (step 3—sideward step).
Drawing by Craig Turski.

Jazz square (step 4—forward step).
Drawing by Craig Turski.

Jazz Square

Jazz Square is a series of four steps. The four steps make the sides of the square forming a box pattern.

Step 1. Cross the left foot over the right. This is the front side of the square.

Step 2. Step backward onto the right (right side of the square).

Step 3. Step sideward on the left (back side of the square).

Step 4. Step forward on the right (left side of the square).

You may begin on any side and then continue through the sequence, but don't cut off the corners turning the square into a circular floor pattern. Play with the timing and facing directions of this basic four-count rhythmic pattern. Stylize it with hip and arm isolations, such as an arm swing with finger snaps.

Jazz Slide

Jazz Slide is an explosive sideward movement starting with a cross step and then progressing to a sliding lunge. Begin by crossing the left over the right. Thrust the right hip abruptly to the right as you skim across the floor into a large second position lunge. The left leg should be fully extended sliding along the floor as you move to the right.

Jazz Slide. Jazz Tap Ensemble with Sam Weber.
Photo: Judy Francesconi.

Exaggerate the outward right side step to create the sliding motion. Tilt the body away from the movement as you move through the plié to improve your balance. The arms are placed in third position or tilted second. Focus either to or away from the direction of the movement by looking over one hand.

Trenches

Trenches are named for the repeated action of the legs which seem to dig trenches under the body. Start in a forward tilted lunge on the right leg. Taking a small preparatory plié, spring slightly off the floor allowing both legs to be free of weight. In a simultaneous action, switch leg positions by sliding along the floor. The upper torso remains fixed in the forward tilt as the legs continue to exchange positions several times. Increase the speed of the leg changes so that you never actually settle into the lunge position before the next change occurs. An oppositional arm swing will help you maintain your balance and add stability to the movement.

Trenches (right leg lunge).
Photo: Bruce Davis.

Trenches (spring to a left leg lunge and then repeat).
Photo: Bruce Davis.

Jazzin' It Up:
Kicks, Aerial Moves, and Turns

Now that you have become familiar with some of the basics of jazz dance, it is time to add those spicy touches that will make your dancing more challenging and exciting. Can you recall viewing a live dance performance or even a dance on video tape or film? What struck you most about the performance? Was it the excitement of a spectacular leap or a breathless series of turns? The impression of energy and enthusiasm that remained most vivid in your mind resulted from the sheer joy dancers exude when they defy gravity performing kicks, leaps, jumps, and turns. Let us discover how to execute some of these stunning steps and movements so that they can become part of your own movement vocabulary.

Kicks

Kicks are leg gestures that can be performed in a variety of ways. They can facilitate traveling; they can remain stationary; or they can be used as transitions to link one series of steps to another. Here are some kicks for you to explore and add to your own jazz choreography.

Hitch Kick

Hitch Kick can be executed to the front, side, or back and involves a double kicking action of the legs. The momentum of this double leg thrust carries the body into the air. Begin with a left step forward in demi plié. Passé the right leg strongly. The force of the kick is coordinated with a simultaneous oppositional thrust of the left foot into the floor. This propels the body into the air. As the right leg reaches the apex of the kick, do a grand battement with the left leg. This creates the special scissors look of the hitch kick. Land in a demi plié on the right leg as the height of the kick is reached with the left.

Hitch kick (the jump).
Photo: Bruce Davis.

Hitch kick (the kick).
Photo: Bruce Davis.

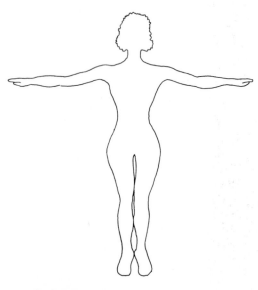

Jump kick (the preparation).
Drawing by Craig Turski.

Jump kick (the kick).
Drawing by Craig Turski.

122

Jump Kick

Jump Kick is a bouncing kick that includes an assemblé and a hop (see assemblé page 138) and must be executed in a demi plié on the supporting leg. They are seen most often in chorus lines. Begin in a closed position. Prepare for the kick with a quick snappy jump with the feet together. As the body rises from the plié, grand battement the left leg. At the height of the kick do a small hop on the right leg. When the kick is completed by the left leg, land on two legs in demi plié (assemblé) to finish the step. Repeat the kick with the right, or, for a variation, jump to a passé position in place of the kick. When performed in a series from a passé position, they are called *hop kicks*.

Fan Kick

Fan Kick inscribes a full circle when the gesture foot passes above the head as it moves from one side of the body across the centerline to the other side. Begin in a closed position. Grand battement the right leg to the left side of the body, then reverse the energy by sweeping the leg across the front of the body to the right side in a large arcing motion. Maximum height of the kick is reached in front of the body. Complete the kick by closing in fifth position or by landing in a side lunge. Usually, you step into a fan kick in order to develop momentum. Fan kicks may also be executed as jumps kicks, and are effective when done in a series.

Fan kick.
Photo: Bruce Davis.

Swing Kicks

Swing Kicks are executed from a lunge position to the front, side, or back. It is an exaggerated grand battement that swings through first position from the lunge up to the height of the kick.

Front kick begins in a forward lunge on the left leg, the right leg extended to the back. Shift onto the left while sweeping the right leg from the back through first position to a forward grand battement. The left leg straightens at the height of the kick. Reverse the action and control the lowering of the right leg back to the lunge position.

Back kick starts in a forward lunge with the right foot in front. Swing the right leg to the back kicking to an arabesque position. The back is lifted and remains balanced over the supporting leg. A strong oppositional arm swing will also help your balance. Reverse the action and control the lowering of the right leg back to the forward lunge. Switch legs in the lunge to repeat with a left leg.

Side kick uses a cross leg lunge. Here the left leg crossed diagonally in front of the right over the body's center line. The right leg is extended to the back left diagonal. Swing the right leg to the right side in a grand battement and recover to the starting position. Reverse the cross leg lunge and repeat the kick to the left with the left leg.

For variety, perform swing kicks in attitude position or with a transitional step between each kick. It is easy and fun to link the kicks together in a series that moves front, back, and then side. The arms are held in a stable position to help maintain your balance, or can swing in opposition with each kick.

Swing kick (fourth position preparation).
Drawing by Craig Turski.

Swing kick (the kick).
Drawing by Craig Turski.

Step Kick

Step Kick is a moving step which includes one step or a series of steps in between each kick. The number of steps between each kick depends on the intention of the movement and the pulse of the music. An odd number of steps results in the kick alternating from one leg to the other. An even number of steps will keep the kick on the same leg. Remember the first step after the kick is done with the kicking leg. Here are two jazz variations:

1. Perform a three-step turn traveling to the front or side-to-side between each kick so that the kick alternates from one leg to the other.
2. Step to the back and execute the kick to the arabesque position.

Step kick (step preparation).
Photo: Bruce Davis.

Step kick (kicking to the front).
Photo: Bruce Davis.

Accented kick.
Photo: Bruce Davis.

Accented Kick

An accented kick is also called a *flick kick* because a quick release with a rebounding return action is emphasized. The kicking leg begins and ends in a bent knee with the leg and foot extending fully for a split second before it quickly withdraws back to the supporting foot. It is a spring loaded flicking movement. For a variation, leave the leg in the extended position and then take a step onto that leg to repeat it on the other leg.

Developpé Kick

The developpé kick is very similar to the accented kick except that the leg is drawn up to a passé position with the toe definitely touching the supporting knee before the accented kick is performed. The kicks may be done to the front, side, or back. However, the side kick is the most common of the three. Greater height can be achieved in the side position with the use of turn-out. For a variation, close the leg to fifth position with a straight knee, as is done in a grand battement, instead of returning the leg through the passé position (retiré).

Developpé kick (a straight leg kick with a relevé and a high back release).
Photo: Bruce Davis.

Developpé kick (in a contraction).
Photo: Bruce Davis.

Kick ball change. The flicking kick.
Photo: Bruce Davis.

The rocking step onto the ball of the foot.
Photo: Bruce Davis.

The weight shifted back onto the right foot.
Photo: Bruce Davis.

Kick Ball Change

Kick Ball Change is a step pattern that includes a loose flicking kick and a small rocking weight shift. The kick is usually executed to the front or more commonly across the body to a front diagonal. Begin in second position with a slight turn-out. Shift onto the right foot and execute a small accented kick across the body with the left foot. Be sure to point the foot fully and extend both the supporting and working legs during the kick. Quickly lower the left leg and take a light side step on the ball of the left foot. Abruptly shift back to the right. This is called a *ball change*. The rhythm of a ball change is always uneven (· — short-long). Repeating to the other side, take a step to the left on the left leg and kick ball change with the right foot.

Airborne Movements

These movements occur when the weight is temporarily taken off both feet while the legs and body appear to defy gravity. Airborne movements are classified according to the type of support at the time of the takeoff and at the landing. Generally there are five

Hop (with a contraction). Gus Giordano Jazz Dance Chicago in "Gang Hep."
Photo: Mike Canale.

types of airborne movements, and each classification suggests numerous visually exciting leg positions and vibrant dynamics. Five aerial movements are listed here along with the support at the takeoff and the landing positions.

Step	Takeoff	Landing
Hop	one foot	the same foot
Leap	one foot	the other foot
Jump	both feet	both feet
Assemblé	one foot	both feet
Sissonne	both feet	one foot

Hop

Hop takes off on one foot and lands on the same foot. You know hops from having done skips, which are hop-step patterns performed in succession. Although a hop does not require a traveling takeoff, the added momentum of preparing for a hop with a chassé or series of steps makes the movement more exciting to watch and to execute.

Some jazz variations in the position of the gesture leg include a parallel or turned out passé, a hitch kick forward, side, or backward, or a grand battement with a hop as in jump kicks.

Here are a few more variations:

1. Turn while in the air, usually *en dedans* (to the inside).
2. Hold the heel of an extended leg in a split and hop *en dehors* (to the outside), performing a *can-can step*.
3. Stylize the hop with an accented heel click known as a *bell*. You probably have seen it used in sailor dances or in various tap routines. Step across the body's center, then thrust the gesture leg into a side grand battement drawing the heels together with bent knees as you hop. Bells are usually repeated to alternate sides.

Grand jeté. Gus Giordano Jazz Dance Chicago.
Photo: Mike Canale.

Leap (Jeté)

Leap, or jeté, leaves the ground on one foot and lands on the other. The most spectacular is the *grand jeté* in which the dancer executes a full split in the air either to the front or side. There are many variations of leg positions in the air, such as a single or double attitude. Remember, all leaps travel through space and must contain a moment of suspension.

Grand jeté is the most eye-catching of all the leaps. To build up your momentum, begin with three running steps, (left, right, left), then brush the right leg strongly in a thrusted forward dégagé. The left leg pushes off the floor to extend fully as both legs stretch away from each other in an aerial split. Land on the right foot as the momentum carries you forward in space. Deepen the demi plié and elongate the ending arabesque position. The torso and focus must remain lifted to counteract and mask the force of the landing. The leading leg may remain fully extended as it brushes the floor, or execute a flick kick first. In a *saut de chat,* the flick kick quickly extends and the second leg remains bent underneath your center.

Saut de chat. Delia Stewart Dance Company.

Pas de chat means "step of the cat." The name is derived from the seemingly soft landing and the catlike prowess of the step. The leap begins in fifth position plié, usually as you complete a connecting step such as pas de bourrée or glissade. Start with the right leg front and snatch the pointed foot up to the left leg briskly to a passé position. As the foot reaches the height of the passé, spring off the left leg. Let the momentum of the lifting right knee propel you up off the floor. Now quickly execute a second passé with the left leg while the right leg prepares to land in a demi plié. Land by closing the left leg in front of the right in a fifth position. The arms can add to the spring of the jump especially if they are lifted above the head during the double passé action. For some jazzy variations perform the pas de chat in parallel position or completely turn around your own axis. This movement is also known as a *barrel turn*.

Pas de chat (in parallel position). Jazzdance: The Danny Buraczeski Dance Co. in "Avalon" with Les Johnson, Rochelle Rice and Lisa Barnett.
Photo: Jack Mitchell.

Glissade is a gliding step because it seems to slide or skim across the floor. Although jazz dancers usually exaggerate it to resemble a side leap, it still remains low to the floor with very little level change. It is also done to the front, back, or any of the diagonal directions. Begin in fifth position left foot front. Strongly brush the right leg to second (dégagé). Reaching a full extension, the leg will be several inches off the floor. Almost simultaneously, push away from the floor with the left leg so that both are fully extended for a moment in a small side split. Complete the leap by landing on the right leg in demi plié and briskly recover the left foot in back in fifth position.

Glissade (fifth position preparation in demi plié).
Drawing by Craig Turski.

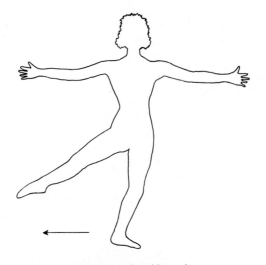

Glissade (the dégagé).
Drawing by Craig Turski.

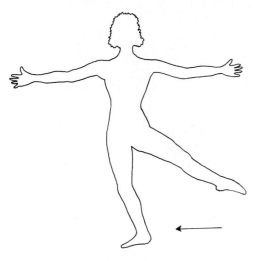

Glissade (the landing).
Drawing by Craig Turski.

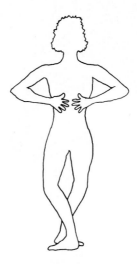

Glissade (the fifth position recovery in demi plié).
Drawing by Craig Turski.

Jump (Sauté)

Jump, or saute, usually begins from a standing start rather than from a moving start. The various jumps are achieved by changing the timing, body shape in or through the space, or by altering the leg gesture. Jumps can stay in place or travel. A basic jump begins and ends on two feet, so start in a comfortable first position demi plié. Spring vertically off the floor shooting through relevé position to fully extend the knees and feet. The stronger the thrust with the legs, the higher and more dynamic the jumps. Consequently, the landing must roll smoothly back through relevé and into a demi plié. Practice this basic jump to develop strength and improve your timing.

Changement is a powerful vertical jump that begins with the right front in fifth position. Demi plié and spring off the floor so that at the height of the jump, the feet are extended in first position. Now switch the feet so that the landing occurs with the left

A straight leg jump. Jazzdance: The Danny Buraczeski Dance Co. in "Blue on the Moon" with Rochelle Rice, Les Johnson, Jim Viera, Karla Kaye Larson, and Richard Havey.
Photo: Jack Mitchell.

foot in front, fifth position. Reverse it by jumping with the left foot front and ending with the right foot front. Here are several other jazz jump variations. Try them, and then see if you can think of more.

1. *Tour en l'air,* a *straight leg jump* with a half or full turn while in the air. You may also add a *changement.* Be sure to spot in the direction you want to land. Add a contraction or arm isolation for styling.
2. *Split jump,* legs are extended either side to side or front to back.
3. *Stag jump,* one leg is bent and one leg remains straight.

Split jump. Jazzdance: The Danny Buraczeski Dance Co. in ''Four Scenes from the Life of Art Pepper'' with Jim Viera and Rochelle Rice.
Photo: Jack Mitchell.

Double stag jump. Jazzdance: The Danny Buraczeski Dance Co. with Danny Buraczeski.
Photo: Jack Mitchell.

4. *Double stag,* the legs suspend in a mid-air swastika position.
5. *Frog jump,* the knees are turned out and flexed and the feet are crossed at the ankles almost like an airborne butterfly sit.
6. *Cannonball* is the same jump performed with parallel legs pulled up to the chest.
7. *Fish jump,* or a *temps de poisson,* springs up and arches the back so that the body forms a slight curve with the legs held together strongly.
8. *Kick hop,* extends the gesture leg to second and holds the position while performing a series of hops. The gesture leg can be held in a variety of positions and the tempo of the hops can vary. The dancer can also turn in place.

Fish jump or temps de poisson.
Photo: Bruce Davis.

Assemblé

Assemblé is a stunning aerial movement that takes off on one foot and finishes in fifth position demi plié. Brush the left foot in a strong dégagé to second position until the foot escapes the floor to gather momentum. When the gesture leg reaches a full extension off the floor, spring into the air. Both legs come together in a tight fifth position under the body. Land simultaneously on both legs in demi plié fifth position. Assemblé can be executed from a standing position and remain stationary, or, following a traveling connecting step, propel the dancer through the space. An exciting variation may also include a half or full turn.

Assemblé (the spring into the air).
Photo: Bruce Davis.

Assemblé (The landing in fifth position demi plié).
Photo: Bruce Davis.

Sissonne

Sissonne is a popular, high energy aerial movement that begins with a two leg takeoff, usually from first or fifth position, and then lands in plié on only one leg. Begin in plié and spring into the air as in a jump. The free leg may assume a variety of positions while the supporting leg extends fully before the landing. After the landing, the free leg may remain in the open gestured position (*sissonne ouvert*) or quickly close into the supporting leg (*sissonne fermée*). Variations for the gesture leg may include passé, arabesque, front or side extension, attitude, or a battement, to any direction: front, side, or back. Sissonne may also turn in the air.

Sissonne.
Photo: Bruce Davis.

Barrel turn.
Photo: Bruce Davis.

Turns

Turns rotate around the body's vertical axis. A wholly different visual image from jumps or kicks, they can travel or remain in one spot. Turns are an important choreographic tool affecting dimension and visual potency of any dance. However, as with the other concepts presented in this book, it will take practice and repetition to master the art of turning. All turns are governed by the basic principles of balance, opposition, spotting, and momentum. Before we begin, let us explore several of these important principles of movement.

Spotting

Spotting is controlled, direct eye focus used when turning to assist in maintaining your sense of balance. Spotting also adds brilliance and visual accent to all turns. When starting a turn or turn sequence, glance at a fixed point at eye level. As the turn begins, maintain that focal point as long as possible, then quickly turn the head around to glance once again at the same fixed point before the rest of the body returns to the front. Maintaining a smooth spotting action without tilting the head is imperative. Practice spotting by stepping in place and walking around the body's axis.

Outside momentum (en dehors) is a force that is directed away from the body's vertical axis. You will feel the energy moving outward from the body's center.

Inside momentum (en dedans) is a force that is focused in toward the body's vertical axis. The dancer feels the energy drawing in towards the body's center.

Both types of turning actions will be clarified in the explanation of pirouettes. For a turn to be successful, you must maintain vertical placement, a strong base of support, and accurate spotting. Review the concept of balance discussed previously in Chapter Three.

Stationary Turns

Stationary turns do not travel through space. Here are some examples that you will want to add to your expanding jazz movement vocabulary.

Pirouette is probably the most common turn used in dance. It is a light spinning turn on one foot around your centerline of gravity (like a top). A pirouette is usually done on a straight leg relevé, but can also be performed in a jazz relevé. In jazz, turns are performed in full turnout or in parallel gesture leg positions.

Outside pirouette begins in a fourth position demi plié with the right foot back. The front leg is the supporting leg and the back is considered the gesture leg. The arms are held in third position right arm forward. Find your spot and push with both legs to passé relevé position as the body turns en dehors, to the outside, or towards the back. The left arm closes to first position as the front of the body reaches the back. Quickly re-focus on your spot and open the arms to fourth or second position to help stop the momentum of the turn. Finish the turn in a demi plié fourth or fifth position. Reverse the action and preparation for a left pirouette.

Inside pirouette starts the turning action with a small right dégagé to the side closing quickly to passé position. The gesture leg can also be pulled directly into passé. For a left pirouette, reverse the arms. The left is placed in front and the right closes to first position during the turn. The momentum or energy for the turn should be directed to the inside or towards the body's center.

Outside pirouette. The fourth position preparation.
Photo: Bruce Davis.

The turn.
Photo: Bruce Davis.

The fourth position landing.
Photo: Bruce Davis.

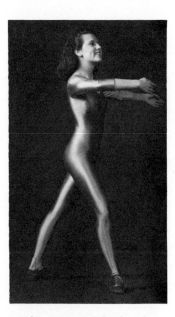

Inside pirouette. The fourth position preparation.
Photo: Bruce Davis.

The turn.
Photo: Bruce Davis.

The fourth position landing.
Photo: Bruce Davis.

142

Pivot turn is a weighted turn where one foot serves as the axis point for the turn. Begin with your weight on the left foot in demi plié. Step forward on the right foot keeping the left foot anchored to the floor with your weight evenly distributed on both feet. Now pivot around by lifting both heels and twisting to the left until the body has made a one-half rotation and is now facing the back. Transfer the weight to the left foot as the pivot is completed so that you can step forward on the right foot to repeat the half turn.

Paddle turn is an anchored turn around a stationary supporting foot. The turn is accomplished by a series of small uneven (— - long-short) weight shifts from the stationary foot to the working foot which is paddling or pushing. The body makes one or several rotations around the stationary foot. The number of small steps it takes to complete one rotation varies with the speed and timing of the turn.

Pas de bourrée turns are performed like the connecting step discussed in Chapter Six except that you turn around within the three small steps. The turn is small and occurs underneath the dancer with very little side-to-side movement. It is basically a backward three step turn within two counts (one and two, — - — long-short-long).

Soutenu is a suspended or sustained turn in which the weight transfers from one foot to two feet. Begin in a closed position. Battement dégagé the left foot to second position while executing a demi plié on the right leg. Rise onto the supporting leg; simultaneously close the left leg into the supporting leg, stepping across the centerline in front of the body. With the weight placed on both feet in a high relevé, spin to the right untwisting the crossed legs until one complete turn is executed. The right leg becomes the front leg; finish in a fifth position demi plié. Remain in relevé throughout the entire turn and spot to the front.

Pencil turn pulls the dancer into a thin vertical line, like a pencil. Step out to the right side into a small lunge. Push up to relevé on the right leg and simultaneously draw the left leg into the right but *do not* put weight on it. The left foot is extended to a low side position as if drawing a line on the floor with the tip of the toe. Execute a full right turn, spotting to the direction you wish to stop. Finish the turn in a fifth position demi plié. Press your weight to forward high to keep from dropping the supporting heel too early.

Airplane turn is also referred to as *arabesque turn,* except that the leg is held at a low 45 degree angle. Prepare with a plié on the left leg and vigorously dégagé the right to second. Pushing off with the left, step onto a straight right leg in a high relevé (*piqué*). Simultaneously push the left leg to a low back extension, turning on the right to the inside, en dedans. The right arm should be extended to the front of the body to counterbalance the extended leg. Hold the left arm in second position. Spot front and complete the turn by closing in demi plié fifth position. You may also perform this turn in a jazz relevé.

Pivot turn (beginning position).
Photo: Bruce Davis.

Pivot turn (step forward on the right foot).
Photo: Bruce Davis.

Pivot turn (step to the back after the pivot).
Photo: Bruce Davis.

Pivot turn (the pivot back to the front).
Photo: Bruce Davis.

Paddle turn (anchored on the right foot).
Photo: Bruce Davis.

Paddle turn (a small weight shift onto the left foot propels the dancer around the anchored right foot).
Photo: Bruce Davis.

Paddle turn (stepping back onto the anchored right foot).
Photo: Bruce Davis.

Pas de bourreé turn (preparing to step on the right foot moving backward).
Photo: Bruce Davis.

Pas de bourreé turn (transferring the weight onto the left foot after turning to face the back).
Photo: Bruce Davis.

Pas de bourreé turn (turning back to the front with the weight on the right foot again).
Photo: Bruce Davis.

Soutenu (preparing with a small plié dégagé movement).
Photo: Bruce Davis.

Soutenu (rising onto the supporting leg and closing the dégagé leg into the support).
Photo: Bruce Davis.

Soutenu (the completed turn ending in a high relevé).
Photo: Bruce Davis.

Airplane turn (turning with the leg held at a 45 degree angle).
Photo: Bruce Davis.

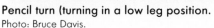

Pencil turn (turning in a low leg position.
Photo: Bruce Davis.

Dig turns consist of a series of pirouette turns that are done in rapid succession. The turns are executed in a jazz relevé. Each turn comes to a momentary stop by digging the ball of the free foot in an open second position. Extending the arms to second position establishes a clean stop. The arms enable rapid acceleration by quickly coming into a crossed first position at the start of each turn. Spotting is essential to help stop the momentum between the turns. During the turn, the gesture leg, or dig leg, is usually held tightly against the ankle of the supporting leg (*coupé*) in turnout or, more commonly, in parallel position.

Attitude turns are pirouettes in which the gesture leg assumes an attitude position. (For a review of the attitude position, see the discussion of the balanced body positions in Chapter Five). Step right onto a straight leg relevé (*piqué*). Hold the left leg in an attitude position (back or front) while you turn. The direction of the turn is most commonly to the outside when the attitude is held in the back, and to the inside when the attitude is held in the front. Here are several jazz variations:

1. Attitude turns can also be executed when coming from a pirouette. As you complete an outside pirouette, step forward onto the free leg in demi plié as a preparation for another turn. Spring into a straight leg relevé and move the gesture leg to back attitude while continuing to turn in the same direction.
2. Hold the gesture leg in a low back attitude (45 degrees) as you turn in jazz relevé. The gesture leg should skim over the floor during the turn.

Dig turn position (starting position for a series of rapid dig turns).
Drawing by Craig Turski.

Attitude turn (the attitude position after the piqué preparation).
Photo: Bruce Davis.

Attitude turn (turning in attitude facing the back).
Photo: Bruce Davis.

Attitude turn (finish by bringing the attitude leg forward to step).
Photo: Bruce Davis.

Traveling Turns

Move through space and involve a locomotor pattern. Most often the path they take is a straight line either to the side, front, or back. Occasionally, however, they will be performed in a circular pattern creating a spectacular effect of circles within a circle. This is more complicated and difficult to perform, so be sure you are confident performing the turn in a straight line before you attempt such an advanced maneuver.

When you travel through space, it is more difficult to maintain your spot. In a straight line pattern, you move closer to your chosen spot. Whereas on a curved path, the spot must be changed with each completed turn.

Maintain an upright position with each new rotation so that the body does not fall off balance and begin to wobble from the desired path. One common mistake is to pick a spot too far behind or directly to the side of the body. Always keep your spot to a diagonal halfway between the front and side of your body in the direction you are traveling.

The basic arm pattern for most travelling turns is to open them to small second during the step and then round or cross them during the turn. The arms can also be held in an abstract shape during repeated turns on a straight line, such as a high or low V position or with the hands resting on the shoulders.

Three-step turn consists of a series of three steps and two half turns to complete one rotation around the body's axis. Step to the right on the right foot, the weight on the ball of the foot. As the weight transfer is completed, do a half turn on the right foot so that you finish the turn facing the back. Continue in the same line of direction by taking another side step on the left, again completing a half turn to face the front. Complete the turn by recovering onto the right in demi plié. Remember to keep the action continuous and the turn rotating in the same direction.

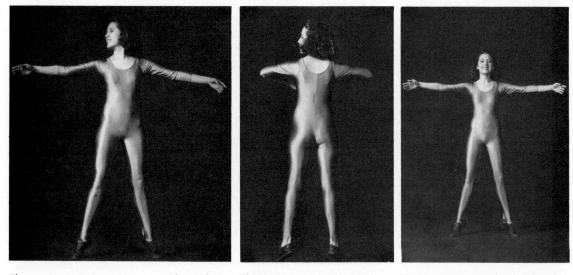

Three-step turn (stepping onto the right while spotting).
Photo: Bruce Davis.

Three-step turn (execute a half turn on the right to face back).
Photo: Bruce Davis.

Three-step turn (take a left side step completing another half turn to face front).
Photo: Bruce Davis.

Chainé Turns are a series of steps that are linked or chained together. These turns may be performed on a straight leg relevé position or in a jazz relevé. Begin with a small side step to the right to execute a half turn to the right. Now step side on the left foot in first position still pivoting the same line of direction. Complete the right turn on the left foot. Repeat this smooth continuous step-half-turn pattern as many times as desired in a straight line. Keep each step an even distance apart, usually somewhere between first and second position. Spot in the direction you are traveling. Repeat the chainé turns to the left.

Chaine turns (a series of steps that are linked together).
Photo: Bruce Davis.

Pique turns are usually performed as a series that travel across the floor on a diagonal. Begin in plié with the right leg in dégagé to second. Strongly step into a high relevé on a straight right leg. The left leg moves simultaneously to a modified passé position (the extended foot held behind the supporting calf). The arms close quickly to first position. Complete one inside turn and finish by placing the left leg underneath the body and landing in demi plié. Repeat several times, one turn after the other. Reach out on each turn; don't cut under. You may also turn in a jazz relevé. Other common gesture leg positions may include attitude or arabesque.

Piqué turn position.
Drawing by Craig Turski.

8

From Studio to Stage:
Designing the Dance

Jazz dance is an art form that is made up of many components: mental readiness; kinesthetic awareness; technical ability; rhythmic structuring; and form and spatial styling. They work together to create a dance. Because you are expressing your inner self through movement, the creative possibilities are endless. In previous chapters, we have focused on learning the structure and technical material that form a jazz lesson. Now let's extend your jazz experience by exploring ways to design your own dance. You already know many exercises and steps, basic building blocks that are used as images from which to create jazz dance choreography.

The person who designs the dance is the *choreographer*. Jazz choreographers tend to highlight specific elements of motion, interesting rhythms, kinetic dynamism or impressions about life that relate to their personal experience and view of the world. In class, you may have already learned sections from dances that have been choreographed by your teacher. The actions choreographers take to arrive at a dance is known as the *creative process*.

There is no wrong or right way to approach the challenge of creating a dance, only the way that best fits your individual expressiveness. Dances are created for a variety of reasons; foremost is the communication of an idea. The choreographer may narrate a story, express an emotion, play with certain gestures, recreate a style from an earlier time, interpret the rhythms of the music, or dance just for the sheer joy of dancing. Certainly other ideas can be explored creatively, but whatever the motivation, the ideas within a dance must relate to the artistic goal of the piece. The art should speak for itself; thus the movement must be true to the idea so that the idea and the movement are fused. For example, in the movie *All That Jazz* (1980), choreographer Bob Fosse created autobiographical dances, which were carefully constructed to reflect different turning points in his life.

Where do we begin the creative process? When movement is learned, we visualize or imagine ourselves doing the action. We gaze intently at the instructor, then imitate what was seen. Perhaps we try the movement again adding arms, or putting more intense energy into the steps. Each subsequent performance of the movement enhances our understanding and clarifies the intent. This process is similar to the child who learns to speak because the meanings of words have been internalized and structured sentences can now be mastered. So, too, choreographers must have a mental image, a concept before they can create.

Imagery inspires the mind and body towards a new way of discovering movement. Images can be mental, auditory, sensory, or visual. In all cases, the purpose is for the dancer to form a common bond with the image so that it can be expressed as movement. If you are the choreographer, you must guide the development of the dance to a visual reality of what has been conceptualized. This is possible because what the mind can imagine the body can perform.[1] How does this all come about?

This chapter guides you through a process that will help you create your own jazz choreography. This process includes ways to define the dance idea, motivate the creation of innovative step patterns, manipulate the elements to give the dance form, and refine and stylize a final dance. Choreography is like constructing a house; it is a building project. First you begin with an idea and then you draw plans and assemble the material that will allow you to proceed to the actual construction. Similarly, the architect carefully supervises the process, making constructional decisions that shape the character and spirit of the structure.

Improvisation: Moving From Within

One way to begin is through a tool known as *improvisation*. This method allows you to become familiar with the choreographic idea by developing original movements through problem-solving exercises. Before the dance is structured, both the choreographer and his or her dancers "play" with ideas related to the central intent. Such movement activities enhance a rapport of mind and body. Together, the dancers and the choreographer seek a common denominator from which they build a foundation for the creative work, the emerging dance. This is where imagery plays an important role. It is a motivating and bonding agent between the choreographic idea and the movement which visualizes that idea. The dancers come to know the way the choreographer hopes to communicate with the audience. They synchronize their imaginative interpretation of the idea with the choreographer's vision. Each movement idea can be mulled over, interpreted, visualized, then expressed. Many choreographers, like George Balanchine, Bob Fosse, Michael Bennett, and Agnes de Mille, have made extensive use of their dancers' intuitive movements as they created their dances.

The improvisational process can be compared with brainstorming. You are introduced to different images which you explore verbally and non-verbally. Responding personally to these images, you sketch movement with your body (like the visual artist

Texas Woman's University Dance Repertory Theatre in Adrienne Fisk's "Dreams and Demons."
Photo: Jennifer Collins.

who makes a number of drawings before going on to do the painting). The choreographer may give verbal or rhythmic cues to stimulate the creative involvement in the discovery process.

New connotations and new relationships to the images begin emerging. These ideas are transformed into movement which can suggest another direction or be broadened into a new challenge. The choreographer controls the improvisation session, perhaps redirecting, refocusing, or setting other limits on the exploration to keep the dancers within the boundaries of the original intent or to see other avenues for continued exploration. You've heard of the expression "thinking out loud"; the improvisation process can be thought of as "thinking out motion."

During these movement discovery sessions, the choreographer often becomes inspired by the material from which the dance is then built. In addition, the dancers' movement preferences and natural phrasing are revealed. In this way, the dance becomes a collaboration between the choreographer and the dancer. In the next section you will find specific ideas that you might use to open up your imagination when improvising.

Up until this point, the choreographer has been making the preliminary framework of the piece; working with the dance, dancers, music, space, and the choreographic idea. Working in this manner helps the choreographer visualize or plan out a clear path of what direction to pursue. Once the choreographer is satisfied with the movement material, it is time to go on to the actual creation of the dance. Some techniques for designing jazz dances are described in the next section.

Elements of Composition: Space, Time, and Energy

Movements consist of three distinct elements: space, time, and energy or effort. You can alter the look, speed, and feel of a movement by altering any one of these elements. It's fun to do this because these kinds of changes make you more alert to the expressive potentials of the original movement. If a jazz step is spacious, slow, and uses light effort, it might look something like A. If the same movement is contained, brisk, and uses strong effort, it might look like B. Or if the movement is meandering, moderate speed, and uses efficient energy, it might look like C.

Let's deepen our understanding of space, time, and energy.

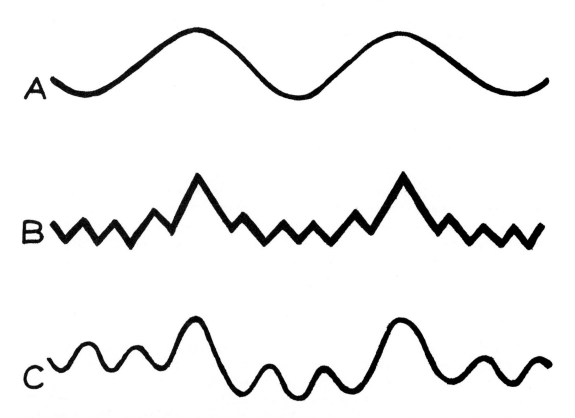

Variations in the movement elements of space, time, and effort.
Artist: Gail Crump.

Space implies the range of the movement. Reaching far beyond your natural range exaggerates the size of movement and consequently enlarges its impact on the audience. Closing a movement into the body's center miniaturizes it. But closing a movement can also have a powerful effect because it is not a usual range. Therefore the audience will attend to that subtlety.

How dancers are grouped affects the audience's perception of space. Think about a finale like "One" in *A Chorus Line*. In that musical, a number of dancers are grouped simply, in a line or wedge formation, and perform in unison. To an audience, that effect is stunning and almost hypnotic in its symmetry.

What happens when the group is broken into individual dancers, each performing a different pattern? The spatial images are shredded, almost like a kaleidoscope. The space is broken up because the audience only perceives isolated segments of the whole movement. The overall effect increases a state of tension, an example of *spatial tension*.

Time is the primary mode of temporal organization. The most familiar is *metric time*. Changing sounds into counts, beats, and meters tells a musician what the sounds and silences are and how they're to be played. Dancers coordinate their movements to the beat, melody, and/or structure of the music. Consequently, jazz steps can be understood by the duration of musical time needed to perform them. New step patterns are usually counted when introduced so that you connect the movements with metric time. In that way, movement, time, and rhythm merge. You want to be "in the groove," to be connected to the rhythm, yet to remain powerfully individualistic. Besides the metered time of the music, dancers relate to two other rhythmic forms: natural and mechanical time.

Natural time refers to the amount of time a movement instinctively takes. This term includes natural phenomena, like thunder or waterfalls, which inspire the dancer. It's a matter-of-fact way of moving, happening naturally as part of your preferred movement style. You don't have to intellectualize or think about it at all. It just happens. Ask yourself these questions: Are you the kind of person who enjoys an even pace? Do you hurry even when you're not late? Are you always pressed for time? Each of us has our own body-mind rhythm that influences how space, energy, and time is expressed in our movements. In harmony with these elements, our sense of well-being is improved. Some variation may give us a sense of energy and enthusiasm. If we have too much variation, we may become tense and overly stressed.

Mechanical time is non-metric, also. Machinery, like washing machines or commuter trains, have a distinct rhythmic time signature. Dancers enjoy emulating these rhythms and using them to inspire movement patterns.

Energy includes thrusting, floating, charging, lingering, kicking, and pressing. All imply drastically different amounts of effort or energy. It is natural to enjoy moving in a variety of dynamic ranges. Energy is the outward manifestation of our emotions, therefore it's one of the powerful ways we have to communicate. Most emotional states, like anger, happiness, surprise, sorrow, and excitement are communicated non-verbally through the amount of energy that is exerted. Dancers call this *attack*.

Southwest Jazz Ballet in "Top Hat and Cane."

How would you walk if you had just won a lottery and were going to tell a neighbor? How would you walk if you were being pursued by an assailant? In both situations, you would respond quickly, and the purpose of your movement would have an impact on the amount of tension in the movement. An observer can understand the intent of your movement just from the effort you've invested.

The spectrum of energy in jazz dance is probably the most important element. How you execute a step and focus your energy often determines the style of the movement. There are many varied and exciting ways to use different degrees of effort to create a unique signature style to your dancing. Observe how others in your class create subtle differences in the way they perform a movement or step. Watch jazz dance videos. Even when dancing in unison, dancers will understand the movement in a way that mirrors their personal style and physical abilities. Michael Jackson uses compressed energy; Luigi's style is lyrical and flowing; Matt Maddox is percussively angular and precise in shaping energy; and Gus Giordano attacks with grandeur and broad power. (See Chapter Nine for more information about these jazz choreographers.)

Regional environments can also imprint styling. New York jazz is low and into the ground. It seems to thrust and throb. In Los Angeles, jazz dance seems to be lightly rhythmic, with more vertically spacious reaching. All styling preferences are valid because they allow you to personalize energy that affects the movement.

Individual elements in space. Jazzdance: The Danny Buraczeski Dance Co. in "Theme and Reflections," with Yloy Ybarra, Jane Blount, Abby Levine, Robert Smith, and Rochelle Rice. Photo: Robin Holland.

Rhythmic Responsiveness: Catching the Beat

Listening to jazz music, as opposed to flat, predictable "top 10" disco sounds, can be a fascinating experience. Virtuoso tap dancer and teacher Paul Draper insists that rhythm in music "consists of visual and aural patterns which live within the framework of the beat and time."[2] Listen actively and certain images will begin to stand out in your mind. These images, tied to the primary elements of music, are melody, rhythm, harmony, texture, and design.[3] Be aware of these elements and signify your awareness by labeling your impressions with selected adjectives. Here are some examples:

Melody—segmented, fluid, lifted, deep, moving
Rhythm—accented, quick, elongated, strong, light
Harmony—intense, relaxed, group, solo, piercing
Texture—thick, thin, hard, soft, smooth, jagged
Design—sketch, construct, conceive, develop, form

Jazz movement is coordinated first to the beat and then to the melody and quality of the music. You hear these elements simultaneously. Which one of these elements will dominate your dancing? Generally, jazz dancers feel rhythm and texture more than melody and harmony.

Music consists of alternations between sound and silence. Listening actively, you can begin to respond kinesthetically. Visible responses occur; the listener moves with the music. Jazz music in particular exploits the body's pulse so that minute shifts of weight travel through the center of balance. Thus guided, the dancer steps just *before* the beat is heard so that the step is made right on the beat. You will learn to control how weight is transferred to improve rhythmic fluency and coordination.

Paul Draper counsels dancers to be active listeners. He encourages them to think out the style potential in the music as the movement ideas in it are sensed.[4]

Listen to a favorite piece of music. Find the primary pulse beat. The *pulse,* or *beat,* is a basic unit of time within a piece of music. Beats are generally placed at equal intervals, but this is not an absolute. Occasionally the music may change speed, called *tempo,* by slowing down or becoming faster. For example, find your pulse by pressing your fingers to your wrist after you have been sitting down for a period of time, and then again after jogging for a minute. You can see that the tempo, or speed, of the intervals between pulses has changed dramatically. Just as a musician may slow or quicken the beat, dancers often sustain a movement across a number of beats or double up by moving faster than the underlying beat.

Southwest Jazz Ballet in "Razzle Dazzle."

A simple value, called a *note,* is given to the basic unit of measurement. Each note is assigned a time value that remains constant. Equally important in music is the aspect of silence, called a *rest.* Since music is made up of intervals of sound and silence, the relationship between the two clarifies style, energy, and emotional qualities, all critical elements. The pulse remains constant and rest values are as precise as the note values. Both notes and rests can be designated as fractions of the beat by dividing them into whole, half, quarter, eighth, or sixteenth increments of time.

The notes are organized within *measures.* This is a way of dividing the notes into units of equal value. Each measure will have the same number of beats, but the nature of the beats in each measure may vary. A measure is sometimes referred to as a *bar* because of the vertical line that divides each measure on a sheet of music. The consistent way the rhythmic pattern of the beats are organized within each measure, or bar, is called the *meter.*

Notes

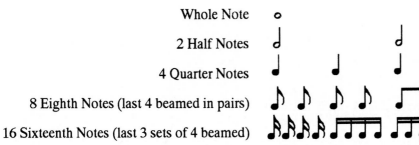

Whole Note	
2 Half Notes	
4 Quarter Notes	
8 Eighth Notes (last 4 beamed in pairs)	
16 Sixteenth Notes (last 3 sets of 4 beamed)	

Rests

Whole Rest	
Half Rest	
Quarter Rest	or
Eighth Rest	
Sixteenth Rest	

Chart of notes and rests.
Illustration by Kris Anthony.

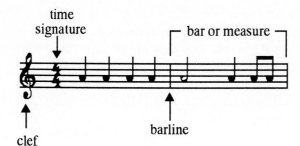

The musical bar or measure.
Illustration by Kris Anthony.

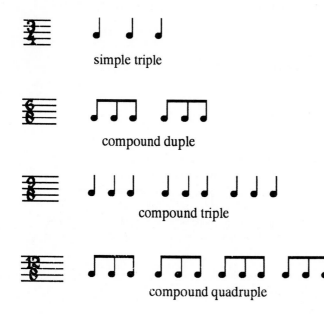

simple triple

compound duple

compound triple

compound quadruple

3/4—6/8—9/8–12/8 time.
Illustration by Kris Anthony.

Meter is the time span of each measure or the number of beats each measure contains. *Simple meter* occurs when there are two beats (called *duple meter*), three beats (called *triple meter*), or four beats (called *quadruple*) to the bar. *Compound meter* takes a simple meter and merely multiplies it by three. Compound duple equals six beats to the bar, compound triple equals nine, and compound quadruple equals twelve.

The meter of a piece of music is indicated by a *time signature*. This device serves two purposes and thus is made up of two numbers. Most popular music is written in $\frac{4}{4}$

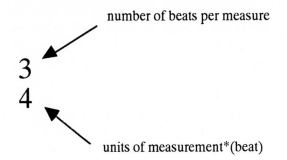

number of beats per measure

3
4

units of measurement*(beat)

In other words, 3 quarter notes per measure.

* Code for the bottom number is 2 = half note, 4 = quarter note,
8 = eighth note, 16 = sixteenth note.

The time signature.
Illustration by Kris Anthony.

time. The top number indicates how many beats will occur in each measure. The bottom number indicates what the unit of measure will be for that piece. The time signature is found at the beginning of the piece of music, and will be placed within the body of the piece whenever there is a change of meter. Musicians, like Dave Brubeck and the Beatles, occasionally change the meter within a piece. This can throw you off if you're not listening attentively.

The manner in which the beats are arranged in a piece of music will determine the *rhythm*. Rhythm is concerned with the timing of a piece, it is how sound, silence, and beats are organized. The rhythm is usually held at a steady pace and we perceive this most often in the drum pulse. But it can be varied and highlighted by accented *pulses* that are felt more than heard.

An *accent* is an emphasized beat in a measure. Most commonly the accent occurs on the first beat. In 4/4 time, a secondary accent occurs on beat three as well. We count it ONE, two, THREE, four. In fact, musicians refer to this as common time. We've come to expect this type of rhythm in most popular music that uses a flat beat. But this type of rhythm is not really jazz! Jazz music is characterized by rhythm that anticipates, re-emphasizes, and syncopates the beat.

Syncopation is a change in the regular meter. It is a shifting of the accent from a normally strong beat to a weak one. In other words, the jazz dancer frequently counts the bar one, TWO, three, four. Through a clever use of rests and changing or combining the meter (from duple to triple, for example) the music may be considered polyrhythmic or syncopated. Dancers mirror this tension and surprise by doing small, isolated movements and catch steps or quick kicks against the beat pattern.

Dancers become sensitive to rhythm through drills to improve their responsiveness to beat patterns. To become involved with the beat, first release needless muscular tension. Once relaxed, the muscles can be synchronized to the natural impulses found in the step or music pattern. Practice coordination exercises. Each time you perform the pattern, release your conscious manipulation of the body. Just let it happen. Dramatic improvements in your rhythmic facility will result in a sensitivity to new syncopated patterns.

Rhythmic training can be a lot of fun. You can feel and observe quantifiable improvements. First, break a complex movement pattern into its simplist form and memorize it. Slowly, as mastery is attained, add another layer of the rhythmic problem until all the parts are learned. See the steps along with proper weight shifts, then add torso contours, arms and shoulder positions, and focus. Never stop the fun by getting frustrated if you forget one of the segments. Make a quick mental note of what part was forgotten, and then go on to complete the sequence. You will be surprised how your mind will focus on that forgotten section. Recalling it the next time the sequence is practiced, you will correct the action. Your goal is to attain the totality of the movement in all its motional complexity and movement fantasy. Learning only foot patterns is exercise, not dance.

Try this eight-beat canon pattern. Reach the right arm directly overhead; touch the right shoulder; lower the arm towards the floor; touch the right shoulder. This is a four-beat pattern. With the left arm reach directly overhead; touch the left shoulder; extend

Three measures of changing accents.
Illustration by Kris Anthony.

the arm sideward; touch the left shoulder; lower the arm toward the floor; touch the left shoulder; reach the arms sideward; touch the left shoulder.

Perform each sequence singly. Repeat them in a canon, or round. The first arm begins one beat ahead of the other arm. Combine the sequences. If this is difficult, go through the patterns slowly. Feel the spatial relationship of the arms on specific counts. Now add a jazz walk in time with the pulse of the music. Once this challenge has been mastered, think of others. Create your own patterns of "movement tongue twisters."

Eight-beat canon pattern; counts 1 and 2.
Artists: Gail Crump/Craig Turski.

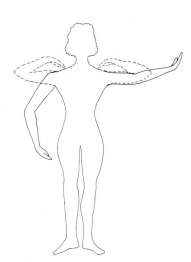

Eight-beat canon pattern; counts 3 and 4.
Artists: Gail Crump/Craig Turski.

Eight-beat canon pattern; counts 5 and 6.
Artists: Gail Crump/Craig Turski.

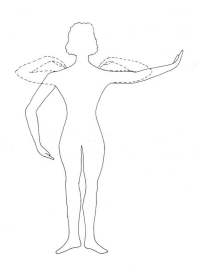

Eight-beat canon pattern; counts 7 and 8.
Artists: Gail Crump/Craig Turski.

Traditional Approaches: Compositional Form

Developing a Motif

Once you begin to manipulate the elements of space, time, and energy, you will discover that there are many ways to compose the resulting actions into movement patterns or phrases. Challenge yourself to invent rather than replicate. Imagine that you must walk through a heavy substance like honey. After you have explored the *energy* you need to accomplish this, change the dimension of your *space* to cover more or less distance. Next vary the *time* you take for completing the movement phrase. Narrow the focus of your exploration to one complete idea. Ask yourself: How is space, time, and energy being demonstrated in this particular way?

The way you interact among the elements results in a movement statement; a repeatable phrase that is known as a *motif*. Motifs occur throughout the length of a dance dividing and organizing the work into long or short segments, much as sentences and paragraphs give structure to a written composition. Joined together, motifs become the messages which the audience looks for as they decide what the dance is about.

The choreographer creates a dance by arranging, complementing, contrasting, highlighting, and diminishing the various movement statements and phrases. The particular organization of the dance gives the piece its own unique form. It's fun to look for these features in a dance. Watch the video of *West Side Story*. In the street scene, the Jets are distinguished by their characteristic jazz walk and explosive leaps. These motifs are carried throughout the dance "When You're a Jet." They are restated, varied, and given dynamic shading as the guys establish what makes them Jets throughout their dance.

Musical Impressions

Music, with its sharp, accented, syncopated, or subtle beat, is one of the strongest motivating forces in structuring a jazz dance. Earlier you learned how to listen actively for and distinguish the primary elements of music. Dancers borrow musical forms to provide a basis for shaping their dances. Some of these traditional forms include unison, dualism, chorus and verse, round or canon, and theme and variation. Recognizing these forms, the audience can enjoy the content or idea of the dance. During the choreographic process, develop a vision of how you will represent the formed dance idea to your audience.

Unison is a form of composition. It is based on an idea that is developed within a single section. We'll call the section "A". For example: A group of dancers are being followed by another group as if trying to escape detection, Jazz walks at a low level in a syncopated rhythm could highlight the intrigue and mystery of the situation.

Dualism is a way to enhance the choreographic development by introducing a new section, called "B". This section contrasts to the first but somehow still directly relates to the theme established in section A. The escaping group of dancers are confronted with inevitable capture. The walks give way to runs and unpredictable leaps and falls in a desperate attempt to remain free.

Chorus and verse is familiar to us from popular and folk songs. Here section A is repeated after section B much as the chorus is repeated after every verse in a song. The chorus can be changed when it is repeated by altering the recurring speed or making the movement motifs more complex. This form can also be expanded by adding additional verses, sections C, D, and so on. Remember that each section must have a thread that connects it to the other and with the recurring chorus.

Round or canon uses a repeated theme that is begun in successive intervals. Recall the song "Row, Row, Row Your Boat." Multiple voices sing one after the other in an ordered fashion. So, too, dancers join the composition layering one over the other, each moving with the same or slightly varied movement pattern. Think of it this way. Develop a sixteen-count phrase with dancers joining at four-count intervals.

Dancer one begins on count 1, dancer two on count 5, dancer three on count 9, and so on. While the concept is familiar, the result is a visual picture that is complex and layered, like a multi-media collage. For a variation, change the facing direction of each dancer or assign each one a different energy and space motivation: Dancer one is excited; dancer two is timid; and dancer three is angry.

Theme and variation uses a main motif which is manipulated but remains recognizable in the subsequent variations. This is a device favored by many jazz musicians like Duke Ellington and Dave Brubeck. The content of the dance is shaped into a theme from which is woven a kind of story. Once an original movement phrase is performed, that pattern is markedly changed and presented in a new way. The new pattern becomes the basis for the next statement and so on. Although the new phrase is based upon the original, the new movement can stand on its own. It is complete. The original statement may never appear again and yet with each variation you can see how it relates back to the original. As in a mystery story, each bit of information depends on what was previously related yet remains unique.

Musical Styling: Listening Closely

The links between jazz dance and music are naturally powerful. Choosing music is a good place to begin your choreographic discovery. The music you choose should influence your ideas by stimulating your innate movement impulses and preferences. Besides relating to the forms of music, as described below, let the musical style itself inspire movement ideas.

Jazz Tap Ensemble with Sam Weber
Photo: Judy Francesconi.

Jazz music evolved in America from many different sources and experiences. It has a long, continuously changing, historical development. Generally, there is a strong syncopated rhythmic understructure with improvisational patterns added on top. This structure is reflected in the distinct forms that surfaced at particular moments in

•

Texas Woman's University Dance Repertory Theatre in Kim Staley's "Mournin' Glory."
Photo: Jennifer Collins.

American history. They reveal an attitude about people and society, and were originally performed with an inflection that has come to identify its characteristics. Following are some of the best recognized substyles:

Ragtime reached its height between the years 1910–1915. It was the product of African-American culture and a changing society. It is characterized by a machinelike duple meter in the base with a highly syncopated melody.[5]

Blues is a type of music that originated around 1900 among African-American singers. It is often slow and sad, reflecting a deeply felt sorrow, heard in a flattened or blue note. But this is not an absolute, as blues can also be very lively and upbeat. Blues are based on the use of repeated harmonic progressions (changing the pitch and causing the sound to rise and fall), and relies heavily on improvisation and repeated variations.

Dixieland is a style that developed around 1910. It combined ragtime with the blues. First played in New Orleans by African-American bands, where it is still popular, it was later assimilated by Anglo bands in Chicago, Kansas City, and other major cities. Boisterously based on a military march, it has a syncopated duple meter with accents on beats one and four of each measure.

Swing was an outgrowth of the 1930s. It quickly gained popularity as the trademark of the Big Band Era. Founded on a two-beat rhythm or two major pulses felt per phrase, it later began to emphasize four beats within a duple meter.

Be-bop became popular after World War II. With its characteristic solo improvisation, using a highly complex rhythmic pattern, the notes seem to continually fluctuate up and down the scale with little attempt to resolve or finish. Emphasis is given to a soloist's interpretation set against a small ensemble rather than the group sound one hears in swing music.

Scat singers, like Bobby McFerrin and Ella Fitzgerald, use vocal nonsense syllables to make quick jabbing points of sound that leap and jump up and down the scale. That quirky quality embodies the nervous tension of be-bop.

Progressive is an extension of be-bop that followed in the 1950s. It denotes a use of some experimental techniques in melody and jazz harmony together with traditional jazz structures. The continuous almost frantic musical passages of be-bop were cooled down to fluctuate less and be more melodic.

Free jazz is a more recent development in the evolving styles of jazz music. Improvisation is again emphasized while steady rhythms and fixed harmonic patterns are largely abandoned.[6] In free jazz, a common statement is made through the development of motifs, usually over long periods of improvisation.

Third stream is a jazz derivative that combines improvisational jazz syncopations with western concert art music. Examples include pieces for symphony orchestras by composers such as John Lewis, Larry Austin, and Gunther Schuller.

Historical Styling: Dancing Through Time

Another way to approach choreography is to formulate a dance around a historic theme or focus on the social trends which reflect a particular time period. You can successfully imitate, duplicate, extract, exaggerate, or abstract the mannerisms of an era in order to situate your dance within a particular time frame.

Be careful to use the movement to illustrate cultural attitudes, not to just present an artificial or superficial picture. For example, to place a dancer in a poodle skirt and saddle shoes may be authentic 1950s costuming, but the theme of the 1950s must also be carried out in the movement motifs and steps that shape the dance. One example is the musical *Grease* (1982), highlighting 1950s dance fads. Consider how the people viewed their world. What did they like to do? How did they think? What were the innovations of their culture? What was important to their lives? These types of questions can help you in the creative process. Consulting films and popular magazines from that time can add to the authenticity and accuracy of your portrayal.

Jazz dance sixties style.
Photo: Studio "Baron."

Jazz Tap Dance Seventies Style. Texas Woman's University Theatre.
Photo: Jennifer Collins.

Endnotes

1. Naima Gwen Lewis, *"Creative Visualization: Maximizing Human Potential,"* JOPERD, February, 1990, p. 30.
2. Paul Draper, *On Tap Dancing,* (ed. Fran Avallone), (New York: Marcel Dekker, Inc., 1978), p. 77.
3. Paul Tanner and Maurice Gerow, *A Study of Jazz,* (2nd ed.), Dubuque, IA: Wm. C. Brown Company Publishers, 1973), pp. 10–11.
4. Draper, *On Tap Dancing,* chapter 10.
5. Don Michael Randel, compiler, *Harvard Concise Dictionary of Music.* (Cambridge, MA.: The Belnap Press, Harvard University, 1978), p. 411.
6. Ibid, p. 244.

9

Cherishing the Past:
Dance History and The Jazz Artist

Today, jazz dance and music embody the American spirit. Their history is a curious story which intertwines the influences of other entertainment forms from the movies to MTV, from musical theater to concert dance, from jazz bands to juke boxes and CDs. Jazz has evolved continuously since its birth in popular theaters during the mid-nineteenth century.

Jazz dancers are tied intrinsically to the pulse beat rhythms and improvisation of jazz music, a "flattening out" of African syncopation, an unusual use of the body, and an interpretive attitude.[1] Let's trace the various threads and memories which are part of this framework of interpretation, innovation, beat, and syncopation.

An African Beginning

Early sounds and movements of jazz originated in the rhythmic call and response of slave field cries and work songs. The relationship between motion and rhythm has bound jazz dance and music to a social environment of youthful unrest. Cut off from their tribal practices, African slaves forged a unique community. They bridged cultural forces and merged European and African traditions. These traditions did not die. Today we can identify such hold-over African elements as syncopated rhythmic patterns and the power of repetition that throbs within distinctive beat and unusual footwork patterns.

The African people were brought to Latin America as early as 1510 when the Portuguese slave trade expanded into Latin American countries.[2] The lucrative slave trade quickly expanded and by 1540 more than ten thousand Africans had poured into the Americas. Taken mostly from the Gold Coast—Niger region, the Africans were shipped initially to what is now known as Haiti.

The finale of Joel Hall "Nightwalker." Joel Hall Dancers.

The Africans' strongly communal culture was largely non-literate, braced securely by oral and ceremonial traditions. Music, dance, and folklore were embedded into all facets of life: worship, entertainment, myth, passage rites, mourning, and celebration. When dancing, the entire body moved; a pulsing torso was accented by a fluent pelvis supported by beating foot patterns.[3] The Africans had few taboos about how the body could express the intent of the dance.

White people, on the other hand, relied more on words to express the heart and the mind than the body. European culture was characterized by restraint and formal interchange. Because the white slavers did not recognize the meaning within African ceremonies, they considered the slaves' dances vulgar and obscene.

Worse yet was the belief that Africans had no culture at all. Their dances and rituals were denounced. Oddly, the slaves were forced to dance these "vulgar" dances during the dangerous journey to the new world. The ships' crews believed the energetic dances kept the slaves in shape and demonstrated good health for the prospective buyer. Many scenes of dancing to the whip have been described in Lynne Emery's *Black Dance: From 1619 to Today*. Therefore, while African crafts and ceremonies were curbed, dancing to the drumbeat and banjo was actually fostered.[4]

Pepsi Bethel Jazz Dance Company in "The Soft Shoe."

Once they landed and were established on islands, slaves were permitted to continue some ceremonial customs. Dances and rituals were adapted for performances on holidays, at harvest time, weddings, and funerals. According to Emery, funerals held special significance for the Africans. At last freed from bondage, mourning was brief. Explains Katherine Dunham in *Dances of Haiti,* funerals were times of true rejoicing. Vigorous, warlike dancing depicted and affirmed community solidarity for the flight of the departed soul back to Africa.[5]

Several slave uprisings resulted in a prohibition on the use of drums. Since plantation managers could not decipher the rhythmic signals, they suspected their slaves of sending coded messages. To make up for the missing drum, slaves began to absorb European musical and dance patterns while punctuating their rhythmic body actions with stomping and clapping. One of the livelier sports introduced into plantation life was the dance contest, where tambourines, banjos, and fiddles accompanied holiday romping. Highly prized were jig and acrobatic dancers who won awards for their plantations.

From these days, three dances have survived. *Buck* dancing is a flat-footed, heavily beaten two-step, while the *Jig* is a brisk, light hopping dance closely related to the *Irish jig*. One of the first recorded animal dances was the *Buzzard's Lope*. Its curiously syncopated brushing patterns were resurrected in the 1920s as the Charleston.

Almost from the beginning then, native dancing in America was linked compellingly to performance. By virtue of idiosyncratic styles, personal charisma, and innovative steps, unusual performers have propelled jazz dance throughout its history.

Early American Entertainments

Until the present century, popular entertainment existed side-by-side with opera and ballet in music hall shows and opera houses. One of the first recorded variety productions was *Flora or Hob in the Well,* which opened on February 18, 1735. That was fifty years before the first star of the theater, John Durang, brought down the house with his flashy English hornpipe routines in 1785.

Next to infiltrate the theater scene were various ethnic dancers. Beginning in the 1820s, European immigrants, who sought freedom and opportunity, were stirred into the "melting pot." Then considered exotic, nations like Russia, Scotland, and Italy were soon represented in the popular theater. Americans were curious about seeing dances like Russian *trepaks,* Italian *tarantellas,* or Irish *jigs.* All were featured as specialty dances in the familiar English music hall variety shows.

Of course the immigrants also flocked to see this touch of the homeland. Detached from cherished cultural traditions and newly Americanized, this audience was curious about American entertainment. Because Black freemen were popular novelties on the variety show circuits, quite naturally the performers tried out each others steps and rhythms. These step patterns and musical rhythms were to become the mainstream of musical comedy dancing, an American theatrical form that was just beginning to emerge. One of the most brilliant and acclaimed stars of the period was Henry Luce, better known as "Massa'-Juba."

Juba dancing was a highly stylized, syncopated stomp and clap solo form. It blended the divergent African and English-Irish styles by *swinging* the rhythm, meaning that Luce's dancing moved around the beat much as a contemporary jazz musician might delay, advance, or slow the underlying beat.[6] Juba was to that time what professional break dancing was to the late 1980s. So popular was Luce's easy style that when he died in London at a tragically early 27 years old, Massa' Juba was already a legend.[7] Read Charles Dickens' own accounts of Luce's performances in his *American Notes,* written after Dickens' tour of America in 1842.

Another popular figure was T. D. Rice. He satirized a lame Negro's singing and dancing and applied burnt cork black face make-up to perform under the name Jim Crow. His grotesque yet lithe characterization was an astounding success. Soon he was joined by a chorus of pretenders, all eager to "Jump Jim Crow."[8] *Black face* acts satirized plantation life and soon became a mainstay of minstrel shows.[9]

Springing into popularity prior to the Civil War, around 1842, minstrel shows came about because an economic depression forced solo entertainers to band together in order to survive.[10] Born on the plantation, the style of these troupes borrowed heavily from country slapstick humor, English clog and hornpipe, Irish jig, and the African derived *buck 'n' wing,* shuffling, and gliding dances. The Virginia Minstrels was one of the earliest troupes and the Christy Minstrels featured songs by Stephen Foster, like the favorite "Oh Susanna." This all-white group sang, performed stand-up comedy, and danced in a high strutting style called the *olio.*[11]

These shows always concluded with a rousing walk-around in which the dancers challenged each other in cakewalk, shuffle, and strut dancing. The wild, high-pitched *cakewalk* finale quickly caught on and was adopted by other companies. Parading around the stage, the dancers stepped gloriously, displaying their fancy footwork and smiling broadly. The *cakewalk* was a dance named for the cake awarded to plantation dancers who could prance along a line with a pail of water balanced atop their heads. Minstrel shows settled into a pattern of burlesquing the "happy" down home pre-Civil War plantation life. This theatrical convention came to symbolize a way of life that contrasted sharply with the facts of slavery.[12]

Katherine Dunham Company in a cakewalk. P.A.R.C. NY PL at Lincoln Center.

Daniel Nagrin's Jazz Styles class kicks up the dust in a cakewalk.
Arizona State University Department of Dance.

By the 1870s, the rowdy, unsophisticated energy of minstrels was stale. The advent of photography around 1850 and the motion picture in 1896 brought a new kind of reality to the public. As a backlash, a strong wind of artistic conservatism attacked the theatricals, labeling them uncouth and improper. With an air of artistic reform, in 1899 *The Musical Courier* bellowed at "a wave of vulgar, of filthy and suggestive music. . . . Nothing but ragtime prevails . . . It is artistically and morally depressing."[13]

By the 1890s, minstrel shows, Jumpin' Jim Crow, and the cakewalk had fallen under the weight of press and pulpit moralizing. But work songs and field cries of pre-minstrel days had survived in the form of spirituals and gospels like "Swing Lo, Sweet Chariot." Syncopated beat music found a home in tent revival meetings, with a foot stompin' preacher leading the rhythmic, emotional calls and responses. There it thrived to be discovered by composers in the early years of the twentieth century, who were awakened by a sense of American nationalism. Anton Dvorak came to the United States to study this new music and quoted these rhythms in his *New World Symphony*. Others, like Louis Gottshalk, incorporated jazz in their music.

Kimberly Staley's "Mournin' Glory" remembers the dramatic and raucous New Orleans funerals of the French Quarter.

In 1900, Americans awakened to their own culture and were caught up in a shock wave of modernism and social awareness. The new century, brash and unpolished, brought with it an appetite for ballroom dancing revues and the more sophisticated theater form, *vaudeville*. The music was the raucous ragtime. Electrifying and brash, ragtime was also banned by press and pulpit alike. Nevertheless, it fit an era of strikes, depression, war, and assassinations.[14]

Housed in honky-tonks and saloons of the red light districts in cities like New Orleans, Chicago, New York, St. Louis, and San Francisco, black pianists banged out ragtime, honky-tonk, and boogie. One of the first true hits was Scott Joplin's "Maple Leaf Rag," named for the club where he played. People did not so much dance to ragtime as listen to it. Ragtime is important to our story because it acted as a bridge between classical and popular traditions. Thick German harmonics pummeled the keyboard in the left hand while the right nimbly danced over the keys. Two musical traditions were colliding: The old oak was replaced by the swaying skyscraper.[15]

The 1920s: The Jazz Age and World War I

define

Following Reconstruction, growing northern cities needed plentiful labor. Between 1880 and 1910 a sea of rural blacks migrated north to the urban centers. It was here that the line was drawn between country and urban living, the old and the new. Ragtime was a metaphoric meeting point.

As a result of this merging, another African-American form burst to popularity around 1912: the *blues.* The blues sparked a new interest in music composition, with its crushed notes packed in an unorthodox 12 bar pattern.[16] Blues has a sensuous, intimate nature that is exemplified by individual singers like Billie Holiday, Big Bill Broonzy, and Louis Armstrong in the 1930s. But in 1919, well suited to vaudeville, blues and ragtime merged into jazz, a pop word coined with the Armistice around 1917.

Pepsi Bethel in ''Snake Hips.'' The Pepsi Bethel Jazz Dance Company.

Everyone, including composers like Erik Satie and Igor Stravinsky, was infatuated with jazz. Irving Berlin, the revered American songwriter, wrote that "syncopation is in the soul of every true American."[17] Middle America was caught between the moralizing sermons denouncing the evils of ragtime and jazz and their tapping feet and swaying hips.

Irene and Vernon Castle came to the rescue! Clean-cut and elegant in their ballroom style, the Castles banished animal dances by labeling them "out of fashion." Society was enchanted by their chic and bouncy carefree manner. Immediately, a demand erupted for ballrooms and bands. In 1919, when the Roseland Ballroom opened in New York, mounted police were called to control the mobs. The black counterparts to the Roseland were the Cotton and Savoy Clubs in Harlem, known for the innovative dances and music they fostered.

Record players had become a reality by 1914. Dancing to and singing popular songs were the rage throughout World War I. New songs were needed, and bands had to be hired to feed the dance craze. The districts where the newly founded music publishing business were housed became known as Tin Pan Alley because of the clattering of sound escaping from open windows in the summer.[18] Tin Pan Alley encouraged the popularity of vernacular dancing; exhibition ballroom teams stressed individuality and novelty.

Because brass band instruments, with their blaring, impudent quality, were a part of the familiar marching band, dance bands favored these instruments. The saxophone, clarinet, and trombone symbolized the Jazz Age. These sounds, transmitted over the wireless, set a nation dipping and hopping to the *Maxie, Tango, Ballin' the Jack, Charleston, Big Apple,* and *Snake Hips.*

Broadway producers quickly snapped up the opportunity to hire dance teams to appear in their shows.[19] W. C. Handy and Florenz Ziegfeld filled their tip-tapping extravaganzas with eager if not well-trained chorus girls. The first franchised dance studios opened to improve the meager dance skills of the average chorine. Musical comedy took on a new and rhythmic life, and chorus girls began learning to dance to jazz.[20] The dancing was meager by today's standards; men and women performed separately. While men appeared in teams, duets, or as solos, the women were herded into dance lines. Divided by height and ability, chorus girls were leggy beauties destined for unison precision work.[21] The *ponies,* on the other hand, were shorter, better trained, and were singled out for solos. Look at some of the early film musicals and enjoy the phenomenal dancing of Eleanor Powell and Ruby Keeler to get an idea of this style. Not until the early 1930s, when Russian ballet master George Balanchine choreographed on Broadway and in the movies, did men and women begin dancing in a mixed corps. (See the Videography in the Appendix for all films referred to in this chapter.)

By 1918, tap dancing had secured a place in chorus line choreography. Instead of kicks and hootchy-kootch, a rousing routine was enlivened with intricate, syncopated footwork. These dances mirrored blues and ragtime and recalled jig dancers from the past.

Lindy Hoppers were noted for their athletic lifts and spectacular specialty steps.
Performing Arts Research Center.
New York Public Library at Lincoln Center.

The Roarin' Twenties

A time of speakeasies and mob rule, a host of black musical comedies were the vogue of the 1920s. In 1921, *Shuffle Along* was a hit on Broadway. The show was memorable for having introduced the leggy, black venus, Josephine Baker. She later introduced Paris to "le jazz hot," and fueled a passion for tap dancing and African derived dances like the *Black Bottom, Truckin', Texas Tommy,* and the *Charleston.*[22]

In 1928, a black solo dancer, Bill "Bojangles" Robinson, took the spotlight in *Blackbirds.* Considered the King of Tap Dancers, Robinson was entirely self-taught, not unusual for dancers of the time. First discovered at age fifty, "Bojangles" was a true legend. He danced in a whole new way. Robinson's weight was lifted instead of flat-footed; his style was light, and so was his sound created by using wooden soled shoes. His finesse of sound was unknown to hoofers.[23]

The 1920s were also a heyday for flash dance teams, like Veloz and Yolanda, and exuberant Lindy-hoppers. These jitterbuggers pranced in a vision of pure rhythm and wild abandon. Most noteworthy were the teams of Buck and Bubbles and the fantastic Nicholas Brothers. They changed the meaning of dance through their hair-raising acrobatic stunts and spine-tingling percussion tap sounds. Honi Cole argues that it was the astoundingly syncopated heel and toe work of John Bubbles that inspired jazz musicians to create be-bop music.[24] The last glorious black musical opened in 1929, just before the Great Depression slammed closed a golden age of invention.[25]

The Debonair 1930s

While dance halls and ballrooms beckoned dancers with prize winning marathons and "taxi dancers" (hostesses) earned a dime a dance, new threads began to be woven into the fabric we call jazz dance. This was the era when people crept out of the Great Depression to face the devastating Dust Bowl which ravaged midwestern farmers and ranchers.

With order thrown into chaos, people were willing to experiment. Instead of adapting to European models, Americans sculpted new forms. One of these new forms was modern dance, at home with the energetic clean thrust of the skyscraper, the assembly line, and social consciousness philosophies of the post-Depression and New Deal eras.

The power of dance as an expressive form was probed. Critic and advocate of the new dance, John Martin proclaimed that modern dance was "the medium for the transference of an aesthetic and emotional concept."[26] This concept was to originate with the choreographer's need to create and express.

From Europe, ballet had brought a clear form. Its technical discipline was paralleled in the jazz music of trained white musicians like Artie Shaw, Bix Biederbecke, Benny Goodman, and George Gershwin. The rise of modern dance and the influx of ballet into New York sparked a renewed interest in Broadway musical comedy dancing which was quickly adapted to film. Everyone went to the movies, so the Albertina Rasch, Busby Berkeley and Fred Astaire musicals had a lot to do with the Americanization of theater image making. Consequently, African-American dancers lost popularity. Like Josephine Baker, many embittered black dancers and musicians headed across the Atlantic where European audiences welcomed the Jazz Age.

For the rich and famous, the place to vacation was Cuba and South America; naturally the tourists brought home momentos. Suddenly, the mambo, rumba, tango, and samba were *in;* the waltz and foxtrot were *out.* Returning to part of its roots, jazz dancers refined and enlarged the scope of their dancing with these new forms.

Exemplifying this new age of show dancing was George Balanchine, a Russian choreographer who arrived in New York in 1934. Over the next fifty years, he redefined classical dancing. His *On Your Toes* (1936) was a rip roarin' satire about the intrigues of

Joel Hall & Vanessa Truvillion in "Nightwalker." Joel Hall Dancers.
Photo: Kenn Duncan.

Russian opera ballet companies, and included one of the first jazz ballets, "Slaughter on 10th Avenue." Coached in jazz step patterns by a black tap dancer, his dances were offbeat and loose hipped, but with concise footwork. Other classically trained choreographers also left their marks on the development of jazz dancing. Some of them were Michel Fokine's stylized dances for the *Ziegfeld Follies,* Albertina Rasch's *The Band Wagon* (1931), Eugene Loring's American saga, *Billy the Kid* (1938), Charles Weidman's "Flickers" (1936) and Bob Alton's dazzling tap routines.

Throughout the 1930s, choreographers thought about the motivation for movement. Then they strived to remain true to that intent. Dancers began to reveal the "inner landscape" of the mind by exploring personal expressiveness and psychological motivation. As a result, choreographers came to dominate the dancers.

Dance and the Movies

While Busby Berkeley and Fred Astaire, pioneers in motion picture dance, were light years apart in the way they displayed movement in their films, both men were modernists. Almost single-handedly, Berkeley breathed life into the movies by enlarging

Fred Astaire bounds lightly with his trademarks: a top hat and cane.
Museum of Modern Art Film Stills Archive, New York City.

and fantasizing with the movement space. Dictatorial, clinical, yet supremely visual, Berkeley created dance extravaganzas to serve his own surrealistic imagination. Filmgoers were mesmerized by his use of precision dance. But his dancers were merely tools for his masterly images. Later, dancers like Jack Cole refused to call Berkeley anything more than a dance director. To Cole, Berkeley reduced dancing to wallpaper. Nevertheless, films like *Whoopee* (1930), *Forty-Second Street* (1933), and the *Gold Diggers* series created a hearty appetite for dance on film.[27] Watch one of these films and make up your own mind.

Fred Astaire's films, on the other hand, set a number of milestones in the development of theatrical dance. A unique kind of genius, many contemporary dancers, such as George Balanchine, Rudolf Nureyev, and Mikhail Baryshnikov, call Astaire the greatest dancer of the twentieth century. He didn't mimic the music but used both the rhythmic pattern and the melody of a song to create what critic Arlene Croce calls "an ingenious, tricky style."[28] According to tap dancing great Honi Coles, Astaire's dancing accounts for "every note in the dance."[29] Astaire knew he was different; he called his own style "outlaw" or maverick.[30] Fred Astaire's imaginative use of movement and props inspired others to enliven movement vocabulary and broaden the scope of choreography.

Like Irene and Vernon Castle twenty years earlier, Astaire personified the carefree, debonair, and above all, spontaneous American mystique. At times the standard tap shoes were put aside for his romantic castle-styled duets with Ginger Rogers. Their stunningly romantic on-screen relationship always came alive on the ballroom floor. They worked together on nine unforgettable films, including *The Gay Divorcee* (1934), *Top Hat* (1935), and *Swing Time* (1936), the last tribute to Bill "Bojangles" Robinson.

World War II: The 1940s and Swing

World War II brought the nation together to fight for a common cause. People endured many personal sacrifices for the war effort; gasoline and food rationing was lightened by Betty Grable pin-ups and big band music. The general openness of society during the war years brought to the forefront a number of African-American dancers. These dancers, whose work had modern dance overtones, were supported in part by the Federal Theatre Works Project Administration.

"Out of the Blues," danced by Jazzdance; The Danny Buraczeski Dance Company.
Photo: Jack Mitchell.

A stand out of the period was choreographer Katherine Dunham. A sultry dancer, Dunham was notable as Miss Georgia Brown in the all-black musical *Cabin in the Sky* (1940) which she co-choreographed with George Balanchine.[31] Dunham's eclectic style blended Afro-Caribbean and modern dance techniques, best exemplified by *Americana* (1938). Other shows that she choreographed include *Tropical Revue* (1943), *Carib Song* (1945), and *Green Mansions* (1959). From cakewalk to be-bop, Dunham reminded audiences of the African roots of popular American social dance forms. Her dances echoed the invocations and ceremonials in which trance and ecstatic rituals became spectacular dramas.[32] She was immersed in her heritage, studying it both as an artist and as a scholar. Dunham is a *mambo,* a high priestess of Haitian *vodun* cults. Her master's thesis, ''Dances of Haiti,'' was the first to chronicle and legitimize black culture. Armed with a doctorate in social anthropology, she has received many awards for her contributions to black dance and for her scholarly accomplishments. Her New York school, open from 1941–1955, was a mecca for black dancers. The jazz technique she originated plays an important role in the jazz dancer's vocabulary.

Katherine Dunham, another American original, defined vernacular culture as art.
Performing Arts Research Center.
New York Public Library at Lincoln Center.

Throughout the 1940s, the late George Balanchine, founding director of the New York City Ballet, was deeply involved in Broadway and film musicals. His curiosity and influence encouraged African-American dancers. The rich interchange of movements, ideas, rhythms, and the special talents of many dancers refined jazz dancing as a form unique from tap dance.

Jazz dancers now moved syncopatedly with the whole body, not merely the feet. The stereotyped kick numbers, tap extravaganzas, and "jive" dances were junked in favor of more seriously authentic American patterns. A common set of themes emerged in the 1940s. Among them were James Cagney's stiff-legged tap work as George M. Cohen in the historic *Yankee Doodle Dandy* (1941), Helen Tamiris' suite of Negro spirituals and her *Annie Get Your Gun* (1946), Ruth Page's and Bentley Stone's *"Frankie and Johnny"* (1938), and Agnes de Mille's striking *Oklahoma!* (1942) and *Carousel* (1945). Ordinary men and women were featured in stories filled with local color. The dances didn't just fill the space and time, they were now interlocked with the script. Look at the dream ballet in *Oklahoma!* in which Laurie envisions the murderous rivalry between Curly and Judd.

Jack Cole led the development of jazz technique in the 1940s. He's considered by many as the "father of jazz dance." Many great dancers and choreographers from the 1950s to 1970s including Bob Fosse, Matt Mattox, Jerome Robbins, Gwen Verdon, Peter

Jack Cole was a "hip master" whose syncopated isolations framed jazz dance.
Photo: Marcus Blechman.
Performing Arts Research Center.
New York Public Library at Lincoln Center.

Gennaro, and Gower Champion, owe their styles to this man. Cole was a complex man whose film choreography never did justice to his inventiveness. After studying with early modern dancer Ruth St. Denis, Cole's Broadway debut occurred in the 1933 production *School for Husbands.*

St. Denis' classes in Oriental dancing fascinated Cole. This motivated him to study with the best teachers of East Indian classical dancing of the time: Uday Shankar and La Meri. Cole naturally swung and syncopated movement sharply, so his study of classical Indian dancing brought these elements into a unique pattern. Later, his dance style evolved into the jazz isolation patterns we do today. Enjoy his athletic zany patterns in *Kismet* (1955).

The 1940s were an important time in the shaping of jazz dance technique. Jazz dance was dominated by the innovations of African-American dancers, refined by ballet vocabulary, and made more relevant by the modern dancers. Jack Cole drew together these factors when he explored the sensitive, articulate movement potential of the torso, head, and arms as well as the legs and feet.[33]

We see Cole's contributions in every single contemporary jazz style. Intensely American in its loose-hipped, finger-snapping jive, Cole never separated jazz from its strong underlying rhythmic structure.

Gwen Verden rehearsing a tribute to Jack Cole, her teacher.
American Dance Machine.

Flexed wrists and flamboyant use of the limbs are hallmarks of classical jazz styling.
San Francisco Jazz Company.
Photo: Blake Davis.

Few women, besides Katherine Dunham and Agnes de Mille, have directly influenced the course of jazz dancing as much as Hanya Holm. Holm was a German dancer who came to the United States in 1932 to teach the modern dance of her mentor Mary Wigman. With no training in tap dance or popular theater forms, Holm arrived on Broadway eager to absorb the unique pulses, rhythms, and characteristics of her newly adopted nation. Throughout her career she developed her own style. She had a solid grounding in Wigman's internal approach to choreography. That is she set out to create a dance by getting inside the essential feeling or dance idea. Her dancers participated in the creative process by improvising until the right movement was discovered. She was sensitive to space and the lack of inhibitions she found in America. To Holm, "space is a living factor."[34] Watch *Kiss Me, Kate* (1948). Holm captured the flavor of tap and jazz dancing while fitting these forms to her own ideas of space, time, and form. With her stylish numbers for *My Fair Lady* (1956), Holm became one of the few modern dancers to successfully bridge Broadway and the concert stage.

Jerome Robbins' rise to stardom was swift and sure. His dances, like the wartime *Fancy Free* (1944), which was expanded into the show and film *On the Town* (1949), are physically expressive. He combines contemporary literal gesture, like a sailor's salute, a shoulder shrug, or a quick finger snap, with thrilling technical movement.[35] Like Agnes de Mille, Jerry "expressed [an] affirmation in things American at a point in history when affirmation of principle was of great importance".[36]

The urge to represent his own era drove Robbins into choreography which explored theatrical timing and common, everyday events. A mixture of various dance genius combined with sure-footed musicality describe the stylish dances he created for *The King and I* (1951), *Peter Pan* (1954), and *Fiddler on the Roof* (1964). Even if he'd only created one production, *West Side Story* (1957) would have been enough to etch his name in the annals of dance history. *West Side Story* was earthshaking in its dissection of the basic energies involved in gang warfare and death. Robbins made dance integral to the plot, something that had not been done before. A thunderstorm of energy characterized the confrontational dances which pit Jets against Sharks and a flat American beat against staccato Spanish rhythms.

Formerly a chemistry major at New York University, Robbins had studied many kinds of dance, from Oriental and tap to Spanish and ballet. He was a new breed of show dancer; not born on the street but coming from a solid technical background. After a hiatus on Broadway of twenty-five years, Robbins devised a stunning, award-winning reflective production *Jerome Robbins' Broadway* (1988).

The Jets take charge in Jerome Robbins' *West Side Story.*
Museum of Modern Art, Film Still Archive, New York City.

Beginning in the late 1940s, we see another man, Gene Kelly, whose enduring good looks and boy-next-door charm propelled a renaissance in the film musical. From buck and wing to ballet, Kelly injected an open collar freshness and all-American athleticism into his productions. Kelly both choreographed and danced in most of his films; his musicals are some of the most successful ever done. *Singin' in the Rain* (1952), *An American in Paris* (1951), and his animated fantasy film *Invitation to the Dance* (1957) are true classics. They represent Kelly's own dictum that "a dancer expresses with his body what an actor does with words."[37]

Most of Kelly's dances were based upon tap rhythms with undertones of ballet. Relying generally on symmetrical formations and a weighted quality, there is little use of the rhythmic isolations which Jack Cole had introduced. Consequently, a trend developed that looked away from a true exploration of jazz. More and more dancers took a show dancing approach that was popularized by Kelly's virile, yet rhythmically flat choreography. Kelly didn't change theater and jazz dance, but he devised imaginative, fun dance fantasies. He made jazz dance fashionable.

Gene Kelly slides with Tom in *Anchors Away.*
Museum of Modern Art, Film Stills Archives, New York City.

The 1950s to the Present Baby Boomers and to MTV

Throughout the 1950s, the sense of cool, hip be-bop of Dizzy Gillespie, Miles Davis, and John Coltrane were counterbalanced by the wave of popular dance music. Out of the African-American clubs and the gospel music, rhythm and blues galvanized as rock n' roll. Bill Haley's Comets and Elvis "The Pelvis" Presley created an environment for the 1960s rock n' rollers who had rediscovered the animated animal dances of the 1920s. The *Frug, Twist, Bugaloo, Chicken, Camel Walk,* and the *Jerk* each enjoyed its day in the sun. By now, television strongly influenced the rise of fad dances through such shows as Dick Clark's "American Bandstand" and "Soul Train" which fed a baby boom youth culture. Yet, except at the discos, fewer people were dancing. Instead of being refined on neighborhood street corners, new styles and dances seemed to hatch on TV. These fads propelled jazz style, then were dropped for the next fad.

L to R: Ron Wilson, Laurie Abatangelo, Duwane Pendarvis in "Changes." Joel Hall Dancers.
Photo: Florence Martin.

At a time when jazz became a defined technique through the teaching of the weighted, cool Matt Mattox and the smoothly lyrical Luigi, Bob Fosse introduced Broadway to an icy, urban fusion of jazz, ballet, and modern. Razzle-dazzle was his look, yet graphic images energized his dancers' participation in the creative process. *The Pajama Game* (1953) and *Damn Yankees* (1955) were two of his early successes.

In an era lacking much innovation, Bob was a fountain of surprises. His were distinct, disturbing dance images. Many of them were gathered directly from his own past when he began his career dancing in saloons and burlesque houses. The longest imaginable legs jutted out from a gyrating pelvis, opposed by sharp, thrusting ribs and shoulders, these were Fosse trademarks. Working out his style on his three sultry muses, Carol Haney, Gwen Verdon, and Ann Reinking, Fosse excelled in musicals exploring the modern woman caught in some kind of a controversial social web.[38]

Today, Bob Fosse's choreography is remembered primarily for its caustic, cynical portrayal of contemporary life and his semi-autobiographical works: *Sweet Charity* (1966), *Cabaret* (1972), *Chicago* (1973), *Dancin'* (1978), *All That Jazz* (1980), and *Big Deal* (1986). *Dancin'* was particularly unique because it had no structured plot at all; it was a show exalting the dancer and the Fosse style. Look to his first film, *Damn Yankees* (1955), for a glimpse of him dancing a stylish calypso with a sultry Gwen Verdon. The Fosse jazz style became engrained on the Broadway stage, visible in the

Shirley MacLaine and Bob Fosse rehearsing *Sweet Charity*.
Museum of Modern Art, Film Stills Archives, New York City.

work of other choreographers like Patricia Birch, Peter Gennaro, and Gower Champion. You can't help wanting to dance when you watch dances like "Steam Heat" in *Pajama Game* (1954) or "Big Spender" in *Sweet Charity*.[39]

The late Alvin Ailey, who began the Alvin Ailey American Dance Theatre in 1958, has been a perennial renegade in concert dance. Critics call Ailey "a caged lion full of lashing power" because his choreography reflects the black experience.[40] His dancers cavort, strut, and bellow in dances which are lyrically theatrical. Jazz styling was an important component in most of his dances. One of the classics of jazz dancing is his *Revelations* (1958). Simple in its form, Ailey used traditional spirituals to ignite the dancers into powerful, spontaneous, and uncluttered movement. Especially gripping is his jazz inspired *Flowers* (1971), which agonized over rock star Janis Joplin's death from a drug overdose. Another memorable dance is the magnificent solo, *Cry* (1971). It was

Bob Fosse's semi-autobiographical film expresses his high-tech life in *All That Jazz.*
Museum of Modern Art, Film Stills Archives, New York City.

made for Judith Jamison, who assumed directorship of the company shortly after Ailey's death in 1989. He dedicated the solo to "all Black women everywhere—especially our mothers."[41] The impetuous *Mooche* (1976) recalls the great gospel and blues singers Mahalia Jackson, Bessie Smith, Marie Bryant, and Florence Mills.

Arthur Mitchell's Dance Theater of Harlem, founded in response to the assassination of Dr. Martin Luther King, made its official debut in 1971. As a ballet company which set out to break the race barrier for African-Americans on the concert stage, its repertoire has always resonated with crescendos of energy. Athough dedicated to the performance of classical choreography, jazz and traditional African themes have been central features of

Alvin Ailey, on the left, in his classic homage to the strength of the early black American church, "Revelations" in 1962.
Photo: Jack Mitchell.

its popular, eclectic repertoire. Geoffrey Holder's mesmerizing *Dougla* (1974) was the company's signature piece for many years. Holder's Broadway hit, *The Wiz* (1975), earned him two Tonys, one for costumes and the other for directing. The glitzy film version starred Diana Ross as Dorothy and Michael Jackson as the scarecrow.

Another choreographer whose work was performed by Dance Theatre of Harlem is Louis Johnson. His driving rhythms and stunning technique exploded in such dances as *Forces of Rhythm,* a stylized cavalcade of black dancing, and in the Broadway musical *Purlie* (1970).

Alvin Ailey rehearses Marilyn Banks, Dudley Williams, and Gary DeLootch for the 30th anniversary season of Ailey's American Dance Theatre, November 1988.
Photo: Jack Mitchell.

By the early 1960s, three men, working independently, coalesced the many influences on jazz dancing. Luigi, Gus Giordano, and Matt Mattox sculpted unique yet related schools of jazz training. While the public was twisting to Chubby Checker's music, the foundations for jazz dance education were being laid. These different technical foundations account for most of the jazz styles now popular.

Luigi created a series of exercises to develop the dancer's concentration and total body coordination. His strong overtone of balletic lyricism emphasizes musicality and elegance along with a spiraling energy that surges throughout the body. Not until a paralyzing car accident in 1946 forced him to find new pathways to initiating motion did this vibrant dancer begin to consider what and how to teach. His New York school opened in 1951. His teaching limits quick twisting or abrupt shifts of weight and posture which, for him, are harmful to the total harmony of the body and mind.[42]

Chicagoan Gus Giordano has infiltrated the mainstream into his style through his long career as the teacher's teacher. Unlike other jazz styles, Giordano's was molded neither on the Broadway stage nor on the street corner. Yet his progressive approach to teaching jazz is firmly entrenched as a popular, uniquely American form of dance, particularly in private dance studios. Formed in 1973, Gus Giordano's company, Jazz Dance Chicago, has grown from a studio-based company to an international touring ensemble dedicated to depicting the jazz dance heritage as an expression of the extravagance and realism of life.

Gus Giordano, master teacher and choreographer.
Gus Giordano Jazz Dance Chicago.

Matt Mattox, who began his career dancing for Jack Cole and Eugene Loring, also helped shape how we learn jazz technique. Making his Broadway debut in 1946, he danced in the film *Seven Brides for Seven Brothers* (1954). Matt eventually set sail for Europe in 1970 where he refined his own dynamic system of blistering, sophisticated syncopated isolations. Mattox's work, described by film dancer/actress Betty Garrett, requires that "you move one part of the body without moving anything else . . . in order to get the kind of distortion that jazz has."[43] Immersed in the be-bop traditions of modern music, Mattox's style also reflects the psychological intonations of modern dance.[44]

The 1970s were set off by two very different Broadway shows: Geoffrey Holder's African-American production, *The Wiz* (1975), a glitzy funk version of *The Wizard of Oz,* and Michael Bennett's trend-setting *A Chorus Line* (1975). Bennett's story was turned directly on the chorus dancers themselves who, beginning by hiding behind their photographs and resumes, gradually reveal their innermost reasons for becoming Broadway "gypsies." The simple choreographic themes never intrude upon the dancers themselves. A blockbuster hit, *A Chorus Line* closed in 1990, fifteen years after its premiere, outliving Bennett by three years.

The seventies also saw more and more acrobatic street dance styles captured and popularized on film and video. Displayed across the nation were individual styles, momentarily spotlighted, danced to Top 10 tunes. Homogenized in form, creativity has often taken a back seat to a look or breakneck action. Teachers scrambled to keep up with each successive fad dance, like the *Stroll, Chicken, Frug, Bop, Monkey,* or *Bugaloo.*

Films replaced the Broadway stage as the model for dance images and style. The flat disco beat and the *Hustle* of the 1970s were personified in John Travolta's macho film *Saturday Night Fever* (1979). Later it was eclipsed in the 1980s by a series of dance films involving pseudo-jazz dancing as a plot device and the dancer as a realistic yet mythic star. Beginning with *Fame* (1980), a lineup of some of these fantasies include *Flashdance* (1983), *Staying Alive* (1983), and *White Nights* (1985), and *Breakin'* (1986).

African-American dance scholar, Brenda Dixon-Stowell, writes that "innovations in lifestyle are mirrored by innovations in dance styles."[45] Partner disco hustle and merengue dancing depicted the sensual, yet uncommitted relationships of contemporary life. Latin rhythms and dances of the 1930s once again spiced a lagging rhythmic base in jazz dancing. Salsa and reggae were the sights and the sounds of the 1980s. A combination of jazz, African, and disco rhythms, this Miami influence resulted in fast-paced, visually exciting dances based upon the *Rumba, Cha-cha,* and *Samba.*

Acrobatic dancing was accepted as another choreographic enhancement with the tremendous, though short-lived success of the Los Angeles Lockers. Their abrupt, almost robotic style was created by their choreographer Patricia Birch. However, nothing had prepared jazz dancers for the break dancing phenomenon of the late 1970s vogueing, hip

John Travolta strikes it big in *Saturday Night Fever.*
Museum of Modern Art, Film Stills Archives, New York City.

hop, and the street funk dancing of the late 1980s. A new kind of street dancing, dancers freeze-framed their actions between quick mechanical movement and acrobatic feats fleshed out with pantomime and audience participation. Dr. Dixon-Stowell writes: "Breakdancing's evolution from street to stage has changed the look of the genre."[46] Spectacularly technical, films augmented the dancing with trick photography which took the dancer to the threshold of fantasy, not unlike some of Fred Astaire's work.

In recent years, companies have emerged that perform only in the jazz idiom. They have injected jazz dancing with personal themes and creativity. Lou Conte's Hubbard Street Dance Company is popular because its serious style and contemporary athleticism are founded in musical theater. The Minneapolis-based Jazzdance: The Danny Buraczeski Dance Company's repertoire is a multi-faceted syncopated, classic jazz style, and as polished and powerful as a silver bullet. Other companies include those of former Broadway dancer Delia Stewart in Houston, Texas; the "refreshingly down-to-earth" Los Angeles Jazz Tap Ensemble; the California cool of the Al Germani Company countered by

"Avalon" with Jane Blount and Robert Smith. Jazzdance: The Danny Buraczeski Dance Company.
Photo: Jack Mitchell.

the traditional Pepsi Bethel Jazz Dance Company; the "bold and classy" Jazz Dance Theatre South based in Marietta, Georgia; the Southwest Jazz Ballet which performs primarily for the United States military; and Gus Giordano's Jazz Dance Chicago which tours his classic modern jazz and innovative works internationally.

Many of the former professional "offspring" are now creating the next jazz era. Giordano organized the first International Jazz Dance Congress in 1990, which for the first time brought together dancers, companies, and scholars to consider the past and future of jazz dancing.

Instead of creating new works, The American Dance Machine, founded by the late Lee Theodore, restages classic historical dance numbers from past Broadway shows. The company is dedicated to furthering jazz dance as an important cultural heritage. The best must not die with the show, but, like the music, live on to be enjoyed by future audiences. A.D.M. alumnae have been responsible for remounting such hits as Gower Champion's 1960's hit *Bye, Bye Birdie* for effervescent Tommy Tune.

"Rose from the Blues," with Ron deJesus and Claire Bataille, choreographed by Lou Conte, artistic director of the Hubbard Street Dance Company.
Photo: Gordon Meyer.

The jazz scene today is now focused on music video productions not really authentic jazz at all but a mixed breed of street, jazz, disco, and hip-hop aerobics with a splash of ballet technique. One example is singing star Michael Jackson whose high strutting style is tinged with rock, disco, and break dancing. His *Thriller* and *Bad* videos have been joined by those of his sister Janet Jackson and Jackson's former choreographer, Paula Abdul.[47]

We can't overlook the jazz inspired choreography of a growing number of contemporary choreographers like Twyla Tharp, Nina Weiner, Eliot Feld, and Margo Sappington. Their work joins the dances of Giordano, Conte, and Buraczeski who sustain the clarity and continuity of jazz as an evolving, thriving syncopated dance form. The future is now bright for jazz dance because people recognize that it is part of a pivotal legacy in American culture. Critics and audiences alike have embraced the expressive potential embodied in jazz dancing, and New Wave choreographers dip into its pool of eccentricities as they delve into modern dance, folk, and classical ballet idioms to arrive at original and often daring choreography. In essence, jazz dancing and music continue to reflect the American soul. . . . Check it out!

"Études en Jazz," choreographed by Herb Wilson.
Les Ballets Jazz de Montréal.
Photo: Andrew Oxenham.

ENDNOTES

1. Paul Tanner and Maurice Gerrow. *A Study of Jazz,* (2nd. ed.), (Dubuque, IA: Wm. C. Brown Publishers Co., 1973), p. 3–6.
2. Ibid., p. 15.
3. Richard Kislan, *Hoofing on Broadway: A History of Show Dancing,* (New York: Prentice Hall Press, 1987), p. 13.
4. Lynn Emery, *Black Dance from 1619 to Today,* (fwd. Katherine Dunham) (2nd. rev. ed.), (Pennington, NJ: Princeton Book Co., 1988), pp. 1–13.
5. Katherine Dunham, "Dances of Haiti," *Acta Anthropologica, II,* 4, November, 1947, p. 53; also Dunham's *Dances of Haiti,* (Los Angeles: Center for Afro-American Studies, UCLA, 1983).
6. Emery, *Black Dance from 1619 to Today,* pp. 185–186; Kislan, *Hoofing on Broadway,* pp. 21–23.
7. Ibid.
8. Emery, *Black Dance from 1619 to Today,* pp. 182–185, 190.
9. Ian Whitcomb, *After the Ball, Pop Music from Rag to Rock,* (New York: Simon and Schuster, 1972), p. 10.
10. Ibid., p. 10.
11. Emery, *Black Dance from 1619 to Today,* pp. 190–194.
12. Kislan, *Hoofing on Broadway,* pp. 18–20.
13. Leonard Feather, *The Encyclopedia of Jazz,* (New York: Horizon Press, 1976), p. 16.
14. Whitcomb, *After the Ball,* pp. 14–23.
15. Ibid., p. 25.
16. Tanner, *A Study of Jazz,* chapter 4; Whitcomb, *After the Ball,* p. 29.
17. Whitcomb, *After the Ball,* p. 17.
18. Ibid., pp. 6–7; Jean and Marshall Stearns, *Jazz Dance: The Story of American Vernacular Dance,* (New York: The Macmillan Company, 1968), p. 102.
19. Jerome Delameter, *Dance in the Hollywood Musical,* Lansing, MI: UMI Research Press, 1981, p. 47; Ronna Sloan, "Bob Fosse: An Analytical-Critical Study," unpublished dissertation, CUNY, 1983, p. 13.
20. Stearns, *Jazz Dance,* p. 147.
21. Kislan, *Hoofing on Broadway,* pp. 43–45.
22. Emery, *Black Dance from 1619 to Today,* pp. 213–215.
23. Delameter, *Dance in the Hollywood Musical,* pp. 79–80; Emery, *Black Dance from 1619 to Today,* p. 233; Kislan, *Hoofing on Broadway,* p. 34.
24. Interview with Honi Coles, "Morning Edition," National Public Radio, July 7, 1989.
25. Terline Terry, "A Survey of Black Dance in Washington," 1870–1945, unpublished masters thesis, The American University, 1982, p. 51.
26. John Martin, *The Modern Dance,* (New York: Dance Horizons, 1965) (orig. 1933), p. 13.
27. Delameter, *Dance in the Hollywood Musical,* chapter 3.
28. Arlene Croce, *The Fred Astaire and Ginger Rogers Book,* (New York: Galabad Books, 1972), p. 93.
29. Raphael F. Miller, "The Contributions of Selected Broadway Musical Theatre Choreographers: Connolly, Rasch, Balanchine, Holm and Alton," unpublished doctoral dissertation, University of Oregon, 1984, p. 246.
30. Delameter, *Dance in the Hollywood Musical,* p. 64.
31. Miller, "The Contributions of Selected Broadway Musical Theatre Choreographers," p. 171.

32. Sally Sommer, "Under Her Spell," *Connoisseur,* December, 1987, pp. 138–143; *Black Dance From 1619 to Today,* Emery, pp. 251–260.
33. Glenn Loney, *Unsung Genius: The Passion of Dancer-Choreographer Jack Cole,* (New York: Franklin Watts, 1984); Kislan, Hoofing on Broadway, pp. 84–92.
34. Robert Moulton, "Choreography and Revue in the New York Stage, 1920–1950," unpublished doctoral dissertation, University of Minnesota, 1957, p. 168.
35. Kislan, *Hoofing on Broadway,* pp. 96–102.
36. Moulton, "Choreography and Revue," p. 253.
37. Delameter, *Dance in the Hollywood Musical,* p. 157.
38. Ibid., p. 205
39. Delameter, *Dance in the Hollywood Musical,* p. 200; Kenneth Gargaro, "The Work of Bob Fosse and the Choreographers-Directors in the Translation of Musicals to the Screen," unpublished doctoral dissertation, University of Pittsburgh, 1980; Sloan, "Bob Fosse: An Analytical-Critical Study."
40. Delameter, *Dance in the Hollywood Musical,* p. 205.
41. Program note.
42. Eugene "Luigi" Louis, *Descriptive Notes,* (Waldwich, NJ: Dance Records, Inc., 1963), p. 2.; Jean Sabatine, *Techniques and Styles of Jazz Dancing,* (Waldwick, NJ: Hoctor Dance Records, 1969), pp. 22–23.
43. Delameter, *Dance in the Hollywood Musical,* p. 205.
44. Elizabeth Frick, *The Matt Mattox Book of Jazz Dance,* (New York: Sterling Publishing Co., 1983); Sabatine, *Techniques and Styles of Jazz Dancing,* pp. 20–22.
45. Emery, *Black Dance from 1619 to Today,* p. 354.
46. Ibid., p. 357.
47. Ibid., pp. 360–363.

Selected Videography

Your jazz experience can be enhanced by viewing a variety of dance performances. Following is an annotated list of films that represent many different styles and dancers who have contributed to the development of the art of jazz technique and choreography. Although all the dances were edited for a film medium, some were originally created for the live stage. Consequently, some of the original intent of the choreographer may have been changed to accommodate the translation to film or video. However, a great deal of insight can be gained about styling, performers, and historical changes that have occurred in jazz dancing.

All That Jazz, CBS/Fox, 1980. (Autobiography of the life of choreographer Bob Fosse).

Alvin Ailey: Memories and Visions, Phoenix/BFA Films and Video N.Y. (Includes "Revelations" and "Cry").

An American in Paris, MGM, 1951. (Gene Kelly and Leslie Caron with a classic George Gershwin score including "Rhapsody in Blue").

Band Wagon, MGM, 1953. (Adopted from a stage revue, it features Fred Astaire and Cyd Charisse in "The Girl Hunt Ballet" with dances staged by Michael Kidd).

Broadway Melody of 1936, MGM, 1936. (Choreography by David Gould and Albertina Rasch, featuring Eleanor Powell.)

Bye Bye Birdie, RCA Home Video, 1963. (A story that is loosely based on the induction of Elvis Presley into the Army; depicts dances of the early sixties).

Cabaret, CBS/Fox, 1972. (Bob Fosse's depiction of a German night club during the 1930s turmoil).

Change Partners, Educational Broadcasting Corp., RKO Home Videos, 1984. (The life and works of Fred Astaire part II, narrated by Joanne Woodward).

A Chorus Line The Movie, Embassy Home Entertainment, 1982. (Film adaptation of the Michael Bennett smash Broadway hit).

Dance Black America, Pennebroker Associates, Inc., 1985. (Currently available only on film).

Dirty Dancing, Radio City Music Hall TV Productions, 1988. (Features dances of the sixties starring Patrick Swayze and Jennifer Grey).

Easter Parade, MGM, 1948. (Film starring Fred Astaire and Judy Garland about show dancers in New York during the turn of the century).

An Evening with the Alvin Ailey American Dance Theater, Home Vision, PMI Company.

Fame, MGM/UA, 1980. (Depicts student life at the famous New York City High School for the Performing Arts).

Finian's Rainbow, Warner Bros., 1968. (Fred Astaire's last dance film, features ''Silent Susan,'' a character who speaks only through her dances).

Flashdance, Paramount, 1983. (A young woman, unhappy with her job, dreams of becoming a professional dancer; features electric boogie and break dancing).

Flying Down to Rio, RKO, 1933. (Film that launched the partnership of Astaire and Rogers).

Footloose, Paramount, 1984. (Story of a Midwest town where dance is banned, starring Chris Penn and the music of Kenny Loggins).

Forty-Second Street, Warner Bros., 1933. (A Busby Berkeley spectacular musical).

Gold Diggers of 1933, Warner Bros., 1933. (Dance spectacular starring Dick Powell and Ginger Rogers featuring the song ''We're in the Money'').

Grease, Paramount, 1982. (1950s jazz style starring John Travolta and Olivia Newton-John).

Great Feats of Feet, The Dancing Theatre, N.Y. (Original film footage of Bojangles, Honi Cole, and The Cotton Club are featured).

Guys and Dolls, CBS/Fox, 1955. (Set in New York in the late 1940s, lots of period dance; a great Cuban dance scene).

Hair, MGM/UA, 1979. (1970 musical based on the Hippie cult, minimalist dance style, and flower power culture).

Hello Dolly, CBS/Fox, 1969. (Set in turn of the century New York with a good use of vaudeville and tap dance to enhance the story line).

Invitation to the Dance, MGM/UA, 1957. (Directed and conceived by Gene Kelly, the movie is without narration and is told through various dance and animated sequences; now considered a classic).

Jazz Art Technique, Jazz Art Productions, 1983. (A video of Matt Mattox demonstrating his master technique).

Jazz Dance with Gus Giordano, Dance Book Club, 1984. (A video of Gus Giordano demonstrating his master technique).

The Jazz Singer, Paramount, 1981. (Remake of a classic redone with a modern story line which depicts Jewish traditions in conflict with current values).

Jittering Jitterbugs, Dance Film Archives, University of Rochester. (1940s vintage film footage).

Kismet, MGM/UA, 1955. (Jack Cole's choreography is featured in the chic retelling of an Arabian Nights tale).

Kiss Me Kate 1953. (Choreography by Hermes Pan, after Hanya Holm's Broadway original; featuring Ann Miller and Bob Fosse).

Les Girls, MGM/UA, 1957. (Choreography by Jack Cole starring Gene Kelly and Mitzi Gaynor).

Let's Shuffle, Dance Film Archives, University of Rochester, 1942. (A rare film of Bill "Bojangles" Robinson).

Lovely to Look At, MGM, 1952. (Film featuring the famed dance team of Marge and Gower Champion).

Mame, MGM/UA, 1966. (New York before the stock market crash. Depicts various dance sequences of the time including the Charleston, vaudeville, and southern cotillions).

Minstrelsy, Dance Film Archives, University of Rochester. (Film about the social and comedy dances of the minstrel shows, including the cakewalk).

Moonwalker, CBS, 1989. (Michael Jackson video of his hit album).

My Fair Lady, CBS/Fox 1964. (Set in nineteenth century England with country and city folk dance and a stunning ballroom scene).

New York, New York, MGM/UA 1977. (Depicts swing bands of the 1930s and 1940s).

No Maps on My Taps, GNT Productions. (Film featuring Howard Sandman Sims, Bunny Briggs, and Chuck Green).

Oklahoma!, CBS/Fox, 1955. (Film adaptation of Agnes de Mille's pioneer modern musical).

On the Town, MGM/UA, 1949. (An innovative approach to a screen adaptation of a stage musical; it was shot on location in the actual places called for by the script).

Puttin' On His Top Hat, Educational Broadcasting Corp., RKO Home Videos, 1984. (The life and works of Fred Astaire part I narrated by Joanne Woodward).

Saturday Night Fever, Paramount, 1979. (John Travolta champions the disco dance frenzy).

Second Chorus, Dance Film Archives, University of Rochester, 1941. (A film about the dance career of Fred Astaire).

Seven Brides for Seven Brothers, MGM/UA, 1954. (A major development in dance theater, choreographed by Micheal Kidd, updating elements from Agnes de Mille's *Oklahoma!*).

Silk Stockings, MGM, 1957. (A screen version of the Broadway show *Ninotchka* starring Fred Astaire and Cyd Charisse and choreographed by Eugene Loring).

Singing in the Rain, MGM, 1952. (Not a smash hit at the time of its release, but is now considered a classic by most critics. It combines dances depicting vaudeville and the beginning of talking pictures with modern jazz numbers of the 1950s; with Gene Kelly, Debbie Reynolds, and Donald O'Conner).

Staying Alive, Paramount, 1985. (John Travolta's disco dance film featuring the music of the Bee Gees).

The Story of Vernon and Irene Castle, RKO, 1939. (A fantasized depiction of the lives of the Castles, featuring the steps they made famous such as the Bunny Hug, Turkey Trot and of course the Castle Walk).

Sweet Charity, MCA, 1968. (A movie version of the stage musical with Shirley MacLaine and Chita Rivera featuring Bob Fosse choreography).

Swing Time, RKO, 1936. (Utilizing a swing score; Fred Astaire performs his only black face number, "Bojangles of Harlem").

Tap, RCA/Columbia, 1989. (This film stars Gregory Hines as a hoofer who is not satisfied with the generic tap of Broadway and features some of the most famous master hoofers of this century including Arthur Duncan, the Nicolas Brothers, Sandman Sims, and Sammy Davis, Jr.).

Tap Dance Kid, Learning Corp. of America, New York.

Tapdancin', Blackwood Production. (A film showing the original masters of theatrical tap dancing).

That's Dancing, MGM/UA, 1985. (Shorts of various MGM musical dance sequences).

Thriller, CBS, 1983. (The music video of Michael Jackson's hit album).

Top Hat, RKO, 1935. (Considered the best of the Astaire-Rogers musicals).

West Side Story, MGM/UA, 1961. (A modern version of the Romeo-Juliet story set in the streets of New York. It's full of 1950s cool jazz and hot latin numbers with a score by Leonard Bernstein and inspired by Jerome Robbins choreography).

White Nights, Columbia, 1985. (Mikhail Baryshnikov portrays a Russian-born dancer who defects and then finds himself trapped in his native homeland once again. His only hope to return to the West is to team up with an American ex-patriot played by tap dancer Gregory Hines; features ballet, jazz, and tap dancing).

The Wiz, MCA, 1978. (Black musical revival of the *Wizard of Oz* story; featuring Michael Jackson and Diana Ross).

Yankee Doodle Dandy, Warner Bros., 1942. (A film that loosely follows the life and career of vaudevillian George M. Cohan superbly danced by James Cagney).

Ziegfeld Follies, MGM/UA, 1946. (Depicts the famous Ziegfeld Follies of the 1910s and early 1920s).